JOHN WAYNE

Books by George Bishop

Destination: Death (novel)

Sex Offenders In Group Therapy

The Booze Reader

Executions: The Legal Ways of Death

The Psychiatrist (novel)

Witness To Evil

An Orderly House (with Beverly Harrell)

Smut King (novel)

Frank Sinatra: A Photobiography

The World of Clowns

A Declaration of Independence (with Allen Chase)

The Apparition (novel)

JOHN WAYNE

The Actor / The Man

by George Bishop

CH A Lawrence Field Book
CAROLINE HOUSE PUBLISHERS, INC.
Ottawa, Illinois & Thornwood, New York

Third Printing

Designed by Irene Friedman

ISBN: 0-89803-009-9

Library of Congress Catalogue Card Number 79-87972

Manufactured in the United States of America

Caroline House Publishers, Inc.

for Patsy

"Sometimes kids ask me what a pro is. I just point to the Duke."
— Steve McQueen

CONTENTS

"If you take twenty dollars and give a dollar to every son-of-a-bitch in a room and come back a year later, one of the bastards will have most of the money."
—*John Wayne on socialism*

PREFACE

This preface is being written on the side of a mountain three thousand feet above the sweltering floor of the Mojave desert. Two years ago, sitting in this very same spot, I first thought of doing this book.

My wife Patsy and myself, with friends Maggie Miller and Jim Ball, carved a mine face out of a quartz vein on this forty-five degree slope. We come here from time to time to dig and blast and muck out for gold and silver, but mostly we come to get away.

As I sit looking down at the parched scrub-covered desert dotted with manzanita bushes thousands of feet below, I see no living thing. The air is clear, so clear that the blue sky sparkles in the sunlight overhead; the soft Santa Ana wind sighs its way through the rock-lined canyons, dried up stream beds from another age. The silence almost becomes a sound in itself, echoing from the range south of our mine.

I gaze out over a vast expanse of peace and emptiness, and think to myself, not for the first time, this is what the critics mean—

without truly knowing what they mean—when they refer to John Wayne country.

I never fail, up here, to get the flavor of the man, to understand what he saw when he reined his horse, and searched the horizon with those sharp, appraising eyes. He might be in Monument Valley, Arizona filming *She Wore a Yellow Ribbon*, or in Brackettville, Texas for *The Alamo*, or somewhere in these very mountains on location; even though what he was doing was make-believe, John Wayne saw the open range, the distant mountains and the vast desert, and, I am firmly convinced, he sincerely felt the impact of what he saw.

One of the reasons, I have concluded, that John Wayne is bigger than life on the screen lies in his capacity to project his feeling for this uncluttered, naive, primitive America onto film, and, magically, through all the mechanical reproduction processes, transmit it intact into our minds and hearts. This highly prized ability is called a number of things by those who would reduce it to definable terms: Charisma, stage presence, talent (although it is certainly more than that), ability to communicate, and, perhaps most frequently, "that indefinable something."

The last explanation suits me just fine. But it is a "something" that really comes into its own in the wide open spaces where the actor and the man can feel at ease.

Have him wear a suit, sit him in a car or room and direct him to adopt sophisticated city ways and you've lost him, on screen and off. Not, as you will read, that he is a crude, unlettered product of some primitive urging; quite the opposite. But his craft enables him to escape the often unpleasant realities of the so-called civilized life and, taking us with him, experience the pleasures and rewards of an uncomplicated, pressure-free existence.

John Wayne has been decried by some, and praised by others for taking this simplistic approach; trying to make it work in his politics and his personal life. Sometimes he has succeeded and other times, as you will read, he has failed, but, as far as I am concerned, right or wrong do not enter into those choices.

It is not wrong, surely, to love one's country; it is not wrong to keep one's word; it is not wrong to make one's own way; it is not wrong to be chivalrous in one's dealings with women. Other people may have differing opinions about human values, but that does not make spitting on the flag, cretinous social behavior, habitual lying, and Cro-Magnon sexual values (on the part of both sexes) right.

This book, of course, was not written in the splendid isolation of the Cady Mountains. I sought out people and did my research in the very antithesis of John Wayne country, in Hollywood, Burbank, Culver City, Newport Beach, and numberless places where information and photographs were to be found.

But wherever I journeyed, I took the feeling engendered by this place, the sense of John Wayne's presence, to fall back on if I needed a little extra help along the way. I hope that the book does justice to this unusual collaboration.

George Bishop
Bloodhead Mine, California
February, 1979

1.

RED RIVER

A film critic once suggested that John Wayne fought like a sissy. Writing of the Wayne-Montgomery Clift roles in *Red River*, Peter John Dyer concluded, "In the end . . . this uncomfortable relationship explodes in the effeminate clowning of a sham showdown."

We can almost hear Duke growling, "Well, I've been called a lotta things, but never *that*."

The fact is that *Red River* represented Wayne at his professional best under circumstances that, had they been known to the average filmgoer, would have been greeted with shocked disbelief.

Wayne was not too happy about having Clift as his co-star, for a number of reasons. Clift was a method actor and the big man had little truck with motivational "mumbo jumbo." The young man was virtually untried on the screen. He was slightly built and Wayne was concerned that, in the fight scenes especially, his solidly built six foot four towering over Clift would make the sequences ludicrous.

Clift's uncertainty about his sexual identity, a burden that was to play a large role in his heavy drinking and untimely death, was known only to his personal and professional intimates in 1948, but Wayne had to take the actor's hang-ups into account; there was the possibility that the chemistry of the two men, so basically different, would prevent a physical confrontation from being credible. As so often happens the audience might be turned off by the picture without really knowing why.

Director Howard Hawks assured his big star that the slim, aesthetic looking Clift would be equal to the challenge and he was proven right. But it was John Wayne who overcame what may well have been a personal antipathy; he generously permitted the younger actor to become involved in his overpowering masculinity rather than be intimidated by it.

The story behind *Red River*, as much as the picture itself, tells us a great deal about John Wayne both as an actor and a private person. Hawks had been peddling the property around the studios for several years. The director put together his idea of a perfect cast. Gary Cooper in the role finally assigned to Monty Clift; Cary Grant as Cherry, the gunslinger eventually played by John Ireland, who calls trail boss Thomas Dunson out and seriously wounds him while being gunned down himself; and Wayne as Dunson. The fact that Wayne was younger than the other two, yet would be required to play a man many years their senior, tells us a great deal about his acting ability nine years after *Stagecoach* brought him, if not instant stardom, at least recognition as a forceful screen presence.

How did John Wayne feel about his role in *Red River*? "Nobody seems to realize," he told an interviewer, "I was playing (Charles) Laughton's part in *Mutiny On The Bounty*. It's just the story of *Mutiny On The Bounty* put into a western and the guy that wrote it did it that way."

Here was Wayne, an actor who allegedly didn't know how to act, cast as a strong-willed cattle baron who, in Walter Brennan's memorable words, "wuz wrong" in his ruthless handling of men, specifically on the long cattle drive that forms the crux of the story. The role, despite Howard Hawks's skilled direction, could have degenerated into a stereotype "heavy" portrayal. Instead Wayne brings off one of the most finely honed characterizations,

John Wayne and Montgomery Clift in the famous fight scene from RED RIVER. A different type of struggle went on behind the camera.

not only of his career, but of the whole history of the western as a motion picture art form.

We are told that John Ford's private collection of movie memorabilia includes a bumper sticker announcing that "God Loves John Wayne." *Red River* would seem to suggest that a big director in the sky does occasionally watch over Duke.

Nothing helps a picture more than a bit of business that catches a critic's eye and gives his review depth by pointing out some philosophical point that has been made on the screen. This is what reviewer Andrew Sarris saw in *Red River*: "The theme of man's presumption in challenging the forbidden barriers of time and nature is expressed most vividly in *Red River* when a menacing cloud hovers over John Wayne saying a prayer over a man he has slain."

Howard Hawks recalled that scene. The cloud was a mistake.

Marion Michael Morrison in 1927, the year he broke an ankle playing football for the University of Southern California. That lucky break may have started the famous Wayne walk on a 50-year career.

When it drifted between the sun and his carefully lit shot, the director was about to call a halt but something (the *really* big director?) restrained him and he let his star finish the scene. The result was not only a visual but, as Sarris points out, a dramatic delight adding an important dimension to Dunson's character. The unplanned event doesn't make Sarris's comment any less valid; the cloud just moseyed by and the Duke happened to be standing there. Pure coincidence, of course.

Hawks wanted Thomas Dunson to turn coward in the climactic confrontation scenes, a role reversal that, he assured Wayne, would be "Academy Award stuff." But the star would have none of it. He explains why in the magazine *Film Heritage*: "I play the scene afraid, but I'm not a coward. If I had been a coward, the kid (Clift) would have been no good because he has to have a high respect for me all the way through the picture. Regardless of my point of view, he has to think of me as a man and somebody that he loves. And he wouldn't if I were a cowardly bastard that had run away from Chappaquiddick."

This from the man who, according to lesser critics, is supposed to know little or nothing about his profession. The *New York Times* film reviewer Bosley Crowther put the Thomas Dunson role in perspective by calling it "a withering job of acting," and so it remains to anyone seeing the film for the first or twentieth time.

*In 1928 the twenty-one-year-old Morrison worked as a
prop man and screen extra at Fox studios.*

2.

GROWING PAINS

A recent poll indicates that more people in this country recognize John Wayne's name and face than any man in history except Abraham Lincoln. So it is fair to assume that most readers know that Wayne was born Marion Michael Morrison, son of Clyde and Mary Morrison on May 26, 1907 in the small town of Winterset, Iowa roughly forty miles southwest of Des Moines on the Middle River. And that's about the only fact that his biographers agree on from that moment until this.

In fairness it should be noted that when a personality achieves the stature of John Wayne even *he* may have an uncertain recollection of some of the details predating his investiture as a public institution. A significant glimpse of how even the youthful, unsung actor viewed such trivia as genealogy and personal biography is afforded us in his answers to a routine publicity department questionnaire. He filled it out at Republic Studios, in 1935, when he signed to star in *Westward Ho!* the newly formed company's first release.

Q: What's your real name?
A: Marion Michael Morrison.
Q: What was your first job?
A: Picking apricots.
Q: What was your employment before acting?
A: Truck driving.
Q: List distinguished ancestors.
A: Never looked 'em up.

The beauty of the man is that now, fifty-four years later, you can hear him giving the exact same last answer. Not many people, public or private, can claim that kind of consistency of character and style. Not that Wayne hasn't consciously changed his image over the years, as we shall see.

However, in those early days the facts of young Morrison's life are reasonably straightforward. His druggist father apparently suffered from both ill health (possibly from a lung problem, a condition ironically to be visited on his son some sixty years later) and financial difficulties; whatever the prime reason, the four Morrisons (Marion had a younger brother Robert) moved to the far west, and settled near the California high-desert town of Lancaster, noted for its dry climate and sparse population. It is here, when he is not yet in his teens, that his future career begins retroactively to shape the public perception of his early years. The choice of Lancaster, barely twenty-five years in existence and set on the barren, inhospitable Mojave desert, portended hardship for the migrants; and, indeed, it was not long before the family again pulled up stakes (perhaps literally) and headed for more populous Glendale, a rifle shot from Los Angeles, where Marion's dad took a job in a pharmacy.

Why not let the memory of the family's noble if futile struggle during nearly two years on the barren, scrub-covered desert rest in peace? Perfectly acceptable if this story is yours or mine but not if it involves John Wayne. Because the shaping of an image is involved, an image that has given many of us comfort and enjoyment over the years. Anything that reflects on John Wayne reflects, in a very real way, on our perceptions of ourselves as seen vicariously through his screen portrayals and private personality.

So it becomes important to know whether, as writer John Barbour has it, Wayne lived on a ranch in nearby Palmdale and rode a horse eight miles a day to and from school in Lancaster, thereby establishing him as a bona fide if putative cowboy, or whether he simply tended the family crops of "corn and peas." Anyone who tries to grow corn and peas in the Mojave deserves a special medal struck in his honor, but no matter; what we are concerned with here is the fascinating process that involved the making of John Wayne and that, inevitably, must include credibility. Not necessarily or even primarily John Wayne's credibility; it is the star system's insidious intrusion into the individual's life experiences that tends to confuse the movie-world observer.

Let's jump ahead to 1930 when Duke Morrison, just one year after his first screen credit in *Words and Music* for Fox films, was signed for seventy-five dollars a week by director Raoul Walsh as the starring lead in *The Big Trail*, a super epic telling the story of American western pioneers. Gary Cooper had turned down the role, and Walsh, who had seen the young man around the studio both as bit player and propman, decided to economize and create his own star. Besides, fellow-director John Ford had used Morrison in both silents and early talkies with titles like *Salute*, *Men Without Women*, and *Cheer Up and Smile*, and gave the fledgling actor a high recommendation.

It was the kind of situation every unknown actor dreams of: The star treatment, big publicity buildup, special classes in knife handling, tomahawk throwing, and even elocution lessons. Walsh happened to chance upon one of the latter and, after listening to Wayne agonizing with the teacher, immediately ordered them to stop; it was Duke's first victory for an image that was probably more instinctive than planned, the kind of gut reaction that was to stand him in such good stead in the years ahead.

Studio publicists could arrange interviews but they couldn't monitor every word; we have newly named John Wayne candidly admitting to *Photoplay* interviewer Miriam Hughes in a 1930 issue that, "He had never been in a saddle until a few weeks before the picture began." That was not the proper image, of course, and the studio flacks soon cleaned it up; in a subsequent interview with the same magazine following his triumphant portrayal of the Ringo Kid in *Stagecoach*, it was firmly established that, "Wayne actually lived on a ranch and could ride a horse before the movies caught up with him."

A small point, perhaps, in light of his career, but one of many fascinating glimpses into the combination of raw talent and artifice that goes into the successful building of a major screen personality. Both critics and public today bemoan the absence of a new generation of truly big name stars of the magnitude of a Wayne or a Jimmy Stewart or a Ray Milland. The answer can be found in the details of how a future star can be isolated from an audience and gradually be given a second identity that blends with but does not intrude upon the basic individual.

Television stars will never attain the instant acceptance and, yes, adulation of a John Wayne because we know damn well whether or not they were brought up on a horse. The public demands to know everything about folks they see in their living rooms, a self-defeating need that robs them of the capacity to lose themselves in their enjoyment. With Wayne, as with other fast-disappearing stars of a near magnitude, we had the luxury of believing numerous little biographical bits and pieces, whether or not the legend was based on fact. Now the luxury has been taken away from us, but it doesn't make the loss any less disturbing.

Take the name, for example. Depending on which press handout you believe, Duke Morrison became John Wayne either because Winfield Sheehan, head of Fox production, lifted it from a fictional character in a Fox western titled *The Arizona Romeo*, or director Walsh named him after his hero, American revolutionary general "Mad Anthony" Wayne (a tough man of action, get it?). Interestingly *Wayne, John* follows *Wayne, Anthony* in the current edition of *The Columbia Encyclopedia*, a circumstance that neither Sheehan nor Walsh probably ever anticipated.

How did the young man feel about the name change? Allen Eyles, writing in his book *John Wayne and the Movies* reports: "Although given no choice in the matter, Wayne has always and sensibly welcomed the name thrust upon him."

But not without reservations. Wayne recently confided, "I never really have become accustomed to the John. Nobody ever calls me

John. No, I've always been either Duke, Marion, or John Wayne. It's a name that goes well together and it's like one word, John Wayne. But if they say 'John,' christ, I don't look around today. And when they say 'Jack,' boy, you know they don't know me."

That is an intelligent, sensitive man talking, one who understands the subtle nuances of the business that has been his life. He may have started out going on instinct, but it didn't take him long to catch on, and to take advantage of the opportunities along the way.

A rapidly maturing "Duke" Morrison has his first screen credit in 1929 in WORDS AND MUSIC.

"He is shy and boyish." — *1930 female fan magazine writer*

3. ENTER THE DUKE

For young Marion Michael Morrison (no one seems to have called him Mike, a more natural but, for biographical purposes, less intriguing name) opportunities sometimes appeared in the form of thinly disguised disasters. After the family moved to Glendale, the eldest son graduated from Glendale High School hoping to enroll in the United States Naval Academy at Annapolis. For reasons never made clear this became impossible, and he entered the University of Southern California where he played football in his freshman year.

By now the tall, handsome, well-built young man had acquired the nickname Duke either as a natural reference to his bearing and good looks, his fighting ability with his "dukes," or take your choice, because he had a dog named Duke. Most fans lean toward the third, more folksy version, an interesting commentary for those of us with boyhood pets who, as adults, seldom answer to Fido or Rover.

Duke Morrison's football coach, Howard Jones, knew Fox star Tom Mix and, through that connection, the freshman earned extra pocket money working as a grip, a kind of motion picture handyman who did everything from carrying scenery to sweeping up sound stages. Morrison was adept at neither. Perhaps his mind was on other things, but legend has it that he first came to the attention of director John Ford by literally sweeping himself backwards into a scene being shot on an adjoining stage.

After the smoke cleared, Ford apparently watched the grip's awkward, but far from obsequious retreat and, always the craftsman, was taken by the way he walked and handled himself under trying circumstances. A couple of days later Duke tripped over a power cable while carrying a scenery flat, and Ford reportedly hired him as an extra on *Mother Machree* in self-defense, although there is no film record of him ever appearing on the screen.

Morrison worked as a grip on Ford's *Four Sons* and graduated to a bit part in *Hangman's House* followed by his first cast credit in *Words and Music* released in August, 1929.

A word about the walk that first caught Ford's attention and has been captivating movie fans ever since. Duke Morrison fractured his ankle during his second and last college football year, just about the time he began working at Fox. It has been remarked that Wayne's walk even now suggests the gait of someone favoring a tender ankle, a supposition, if true, that would make his football injury a truly lucky break. Beyond dispute, however, is the fact that almost everything about the John Wayne we know today is the result of an alert young actor watching, and learning while taking for his own the traits and mannerisms that would best enhance his gradually emerging screen image.

Early in his career, between 1933 and 1935, Wayne did a six-feature series of westerns for Warners, four as remakes of silent-screen star Ken Maynard's pictures. The Duke was thrown into constant contact with an outstanding rodeo rider and stunt man named Yakima Canutt who, according to all accounts, talked like John Wayne before Wayne talked that way. The star himself admits an early admiration for the real thing as far as movie cowboys went, schooling himself to talk "the way Yak talks" and projecting an air of quiet strength. Make no mistake, that figure striding horseless across the flatlands in *Hondo*, or exhorting his enemies to "fill your hands" in *True Grit*, is the result of careful self-sculpting, as though Wayne had taken the impressive basic dimensions of his own personality and physique, then molded them into the ultimate screen personality.

Interviewed at Wright State University in Dayton, Ohio in 1975, he talked about the way he talked. "You say 'I think I'll . . .' now they're looking at you, and you can stand there for twenty minutes before you say, 'go to town.' If you say it normally, 'I think I'll go to town. Um. Then we can go over and see something,' the audience would have left you.

"But if you say, 'I think I'll go (pause) to town, and I'll (pause) see those broads,' now they're waiting for you. So that's where those bastards that try to imitate me . . . they don't know what I've done to establish a thing where I can take all the time I want. (This last said very slowly) I know what I'm doing!" (Laughs loudly.)

But in the beginning he didn't really know what he was doing, and had to rely on his natural equipment to carry him past critics and interviewers. From the start it was no contest.

"He is shy, boyish, with some of the appeal that made Charlie Farrell such a delight to fans," wrote one female interviewer in 1930. "And he didn't want to be an actor. That is the kind of man to watch out for. Remember the fellow that you coaxed into the poker game? He walked off with the money, didn't he?"

She asked the young man if he would let success change him.

"I think," Duke said earnestly, "that I've got sense enough to keep myself level-headed."

But that same rugged masculinity that made him attractive to women magazine writers and movie-goers alike, kept threatening his ability to keep himself "level-headed." By all accounts from the very earliest days actresses who appeared with him in pictures tended to want to appear with him privately, a circumstance that he did little to discourage. Which was just fine, as Wayne himself might say, so long as he wasn't dry-gulched by a jealous suitor. Which is just what happened, and the experience very nearly cost him his career.

Introducing John Wayne, star of his first big picture—and his first big failure—THE BIG TRAIL in 1930.

"Keep your pants buttoned at my studio." — Harry Cohn, President, Columbia Pictures

4.

FIRST FAILURE

Despite Raoul Walsh's direction, a big budget, a great location, and much pre-release hoopla, John Wayne's starring role in *The Big Trail* wasn't a very successful debut. Pairing him with Marguerite Churchill, one of the screen's most established stars, for added protection, didn't help the picture win the acceptance of the general public. Wayne's performance, although praised by The *New York Times* as "pleasantly natural" was something less than electric, and the instant stardom that he hoped for failed to materialize.

One reason the picture didn't do well was that it was released in two versions, the conventional 35 mm print size and a very large 70 mm negative called Fox Grandeur. Theater owners had recently gone to great expense to wire their houses for sound and were unwilling to commit themselves to the special projection equipment required to show Fox Grandeur. Twenty years later Fox tried again and had better luck with Cinemascope and *The Robe*, but that didn't help *The Big Trail* and its disappointed star. It must also be noted that the picture did play on conventional screens without Wayne setting the world on fire; in fairness it was a large burden to thrust on a very inexperienced actor who was struggling to find his identity as a performer. Perhaps the fact that he had diarrhea through three full weeks of location shooting affected his performance. He was very weak and struggling to get through the physical action.

The studio dressed him in buckskin, gave him some props and sent him out on a personal appearance tour, billed as a real cowboy. He quit halfway through, feeling ridiculous waving a hatchet around on stage, and aiming a muzzle-loading rifle. He didn't think of himself as a cowboy (despite his youthful horse-manship on the Lancaster ranch?) and could not or would not carry off the deception.

Today, of course, it would be practically impossible *not* to think of him as a cowboy, which tells us a great deal about the sometimes painfully slow evolution from handsome stud to American folk-hero. Along about 1939, when he made *Stagecoach*, another American legend was making swift inroads into the public consciousness as Frank Sinatra sang with the Harry James and Tommy Dorsey bands. This writer, watching Sinatra sing on stage, asked a nearby musician what, in his opinion, made the singer so different, so magnetic. "The little guy believes it," the sideman answered simply, as the song's lyrics sent the crowd into a frenzy. And that's what happened to the big guy about the same time: He began to believe that he was what he portrayed on the screen and the rest of us believed it, too.

But *Stagecoach* was eight years away when Fox, dismayed by the failure of *The Big Trail*, cast Wayne in contemporary roles as the strong, silent type whom the girls went for. The girls included Virginia Cherrill in *Girls Demand Excitement*, and cute newcomer Loretta Young in *Three Girls Lost*, both released in 1931; then, so was John Wayne as Fox failed to renew his contract.

The young actor seemed at best to be heading for the kind of "B" movie lead career that sustained actors like John Carroll and Bruce Bennett through the bottom half of innumerable double bills; at

Stressing the intellectual side, the cigarette meant sophistication.
Taken about the time he nearly threw Columbia's
Harry Cohn through a window.

worst he was in danger of completely losing his tenuous hold on a
fickle audience. A six-month contract with Columbia in 1931 appeared to be a step up, especially when they co-starred him with one
of their top stars, Laura LaPlante, in *Men Are Like That*.

In hindsight there is no telling how our hero would have fared
had he not been bushwhacked by none other than the studio head
himself, Harry Cohn. Another Hollywood legend in the making,
Cohn was crass and tempestuous even then; he had word that
there was drinking and carousing on the sound stages, and that at
least some of the spirited byplay involved newly signed contract

player John Wayne and a comely young actress in whom Cohn had taken a very personal interest.

A terse edict came down to Wayne from the executive offices: "Keep your pants buttoned at my studio." How did the young actor take it? More than forty years later he talks about the confrontation to writer Scott Eyman in the magazine *Focus On Film*:

"Harry Cohn had taken a dislike to me and was trying to keep me out of pictures," Wayne recalled. "For a year I couldn't get work and I was thinking of going into the fight racket, which I was too old for.

"He thought I'd had something to do with his personal life, which was a goddamn lie. I resented, resented to the point of throwing him out the goddamn window."

But the harsh realities of the studio power structure prevailed and Wayne suddenly found himself cast in "B" westerns like *Range Feud* starring Buck Jones, and *Texas Cyclone* starring Tim McCoy in which he had only a couple of lines. The clincher came when he was called to appear on the set of *The Deceiver*, a thriller starring Ian Keith, who had had a supporting role in *The Big Trail*. Keith's character was found dead with a knife in his back and Wayne was asked to "stand in" as the corpse! In later years when he became the most super of stars, he worked for every major studio—except Columbia.

5.

THE INDIAN WARS

Things didn't get any better when Wayne moved to "Poverty Row," Hollywood's name for a group of small companies turning out cheap "B" product, often filmed in less time than it takes to shoot the average half-hour television show today. He made three serials for Mascot Pictures, a company that specialized in what can best be termed "BB" movies. These were aimed at the lower half of "B" picture double bills, released without publicity to fill screen time, and expected to return a quick profit. Interestingly enough the public became addicted to these cheapies—the 1930s' versions of television's daytime soaps—and theater attendance was often decided not by the feature picture but by which house was playing the latest episode of *Shadow of the Eagle*, Wayne's first for Mascot.

Those were difficult, discouraging days for the future star. True, he was learning his craft and, unbeknownst to him, his one-time mentor John Ford was patiently watching him serve his apprenticeship, waiting for the right combination of movie script and player maturity that would give John Wayne a second chance at stardom. For Duke those were rough days as he was cast in lower and lower budget pictures shot with increasing speed.

"I think I've had more bad pictures," he recalls, "than anybody who has survived in Hollywood. In western quickies . . . you not only try to act and try to keep your dialogue from sounding as phony as it is, but you take a real physical beating in them and you do it all in a few days. Then maybe you get half a week's layoff, and you're back in another."

The serial plots were basically similar, with locales changed to give them identity. In *Shadow of the Eagle* the Eagle is a sinister character who threatens the destruction of large corporations by piloting his own plane and skywriting his intentions. Nathan Gregory, played by Edward Hearn, the owner of a large traveling carnival, is suspected of being the Eagle. Wayne plays Craig McCoy, a daredevil pilot who eventually unmasks the real Eagle and marries Gregory's daughter, Jean, played by Dorothy Gulliver.

In the second serial, *The Hurricane Express*, the villain is called The Wrecker and his target is a railroad company. Wayne plays the son of a man killed in one of the train wrecks caused by The Wrecker, goes on to expose the villain, and avenge his father's death. A third serial, *The Three Musketeers*, has Wayne back as a pilot rescuing three foreign legionnaires from the clutches of some burnoused bandits in the Sahara desert. The rescued Musketeers help Wayne knock off the mysterious El Shasta, bent on wiping out the entire foreign legion, no less.

All three Mascot serials were made between 1932 and the middle of 1933 when Wayne was signed by Warner Brothers, a definite step up, to star in a series of six westerns designed to compete with rising Paramount western star Randolph Scott whose pictures were proving to be big box-office hits. The four remakes of Ken Maynard silents already mentioned were chosen for two reasons: Their story lines were proven attractions, and they enabled Warners to use expensive and impressive location

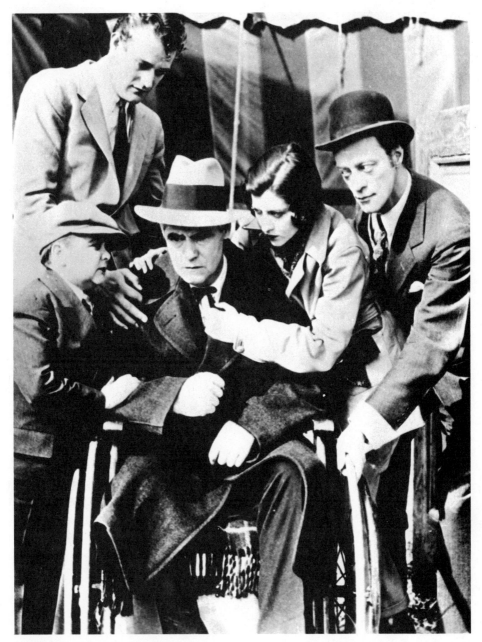

On Hollywood's "Poverty Row" in the serial
SHADOW OF THE EAGLE in 1932 with Edward Hearn (seated),
Little Billy, and Dorothy Gulliver.

footage from the earlier versions. Wayne and the other principals were dressed to look like the earlier players so that even Maynard medium shots could be used.

The most interesting thing about these six pictures was not that they were well received, and represented a welcome career boost for Wayne, but that for the first time we can detect John Wayne as we now know him, beginning to take a recognizable form. The quality of the pictures undoubtedly helped the process. A critic wrote of *Ride Him, Cowboy*, the first: "The familiar ingredients have been mixed with skill, and the fast pace at which the story unfolds cleverly cloaks the obvious. The horsemanship is excellent, the humor is well above average, and the atmosphere is good in detail." (This last despite the use of different quality and different speed Maynard vintage-film clips.)

Wayne began to have things go a little his way at Warners. First of all his more or less casual relationship with Yakima Canutt, the rodeo rider and stunt man, blossomed professionally so that the above critic's reference to horsemanship might well have included stunts. The Wayne image began to be impressed on his expanding group of fans through both his expert riding and spectacular scenes of personal derring-do, largely doubled by Canutt. As we have seen, about this time he began to consciously imitate Canutt's natural way of projecting quiet authority through his speech pattern.

Wayne also rode a white horse through the six pictures, a noble nag named Duke who did everything from biting the bad guys to kicking Indians. But the most important development was that all six characters played by Wayne had John as a first name, a form of audience identification that can hardly have been accidental. Here, for the first time, an identifiable screen personality started to talk slow and walk . . . well, walk like John Wayne. He also had a few light comedy lines and played the harmonica, clearly the broadening of what had been largely one-dimensional screen roles.

The Telegraph Trail, the third in the Warner series, also marked the beginning of what has become the *real* battle between John Wayne and the Indians. In this picture, filmed in 1933, Wayne is a U.S. army scout, John Trent, out for revenge on a group of marauding Indians (led by Yakima Canutt who, in addition to

A step up to Warner Bros. in 1933. His first marriage and a starring role in RIDE HIM, COWBOY on a horse named "Duke."

stunt and doubling duties, frequently appeared in minor roles in Wayne movies) who have killed a friend of his. "Those red devils," Wayne snarls through gritted teeth.

It was inevitable, given our cultural heritage and the screenwriters' imaginations, that John Wayne would confront and occasionally harm Indians. When he strides up to a still-smoking farmhouse, pulls an arrow out of the farmer's corpse, checks the feather decorations on the bloody end, and growls "Comanche," we *know* that one or several luckless redskins are going to bite the dust. Which was fine before the descendants of those "red devils" began going to court to establish their rights, one of which was not to be treated as a kind of American mafia, sitting (or running) targets for the good guys.

The modern Indians began to get on John Wayne's case. The more prominent he became, the more the Indian movement exploited the opportunity to present their side of the story.

Wayne's side is very simply expressed in an interview printed in the magazine *Focus on Film*. "Now, I've done as much as any man to give human dignity to the Indian. My Indian in *Hondo* was a great guy, my Indian in *Fort Apache* was a great guy. I assume the Indians know that I have a great deal of respect for them."

The star has often emphasized the value he places on one human's respect for another as an individual. "Human dignity is the most important thing in a man," he told an interviewer, and it would be safe to assume that he truly feels that way about American Indians. He also has a penchant for speaking out when he feels that he is being subjected to nonsensical questioning, giving the resentful interviewer an opportunity to turn the star's frankness against him.

For example, a *Playboy* magazine interviewer asked him: "What do you think about the Indians taking over Alcatraz?"

Wayne recalls his reaction. "Well, it's such a ridiculous thing. What did he want, a serious comment about the thing? So I said, 'Let them have it. Nobody that ever lived there wants to go back and none of the guards want it. I think they ought to pay for it, just like we paid for Manhattan. And I hope they've been careful with their wampum.' "

It was an answer that matched the question, but it was inserted into the overall interview in a manner that made Wayne look bad. And the Indian movement war-whooped their anger in the pages of the nation's press.

In *Fort Apache* (1948) Wayne as Captain York tells Henry Fonda as Colonel Thursday his opinion of their foe Cochise whom Fonda has tried by force to return to a government reservation. "If you can assure him of decent treatment," Wayne tells his superior, "he will lead his tribe back to the reservation. He has outfought us. He has outgeneraled us. There are not enough troops here to *make* him—but maybe we could persuade him." All the elements of dignity and respect are there yet, as in his politics, Wayne's Indian critics choose to remember only what will draw attention to themselves at his expense.

Wayne returns to the treatment of the Indian in *Hondo*, filmed in 1953 and considered by many fans to feature one of his best screen portrayals. "At the finish of the picture," Wayne tells us, "the Indian is dead—it was an impersonal thing. And I'm saying, 'Yea, he's gone, things changed. It's a good life, sorry to see it go.' It was not saying, 'Oh, that dirty scavenger son-of-a-bitch.' It was a compliment to the savagery of the time. It took no dignity away from any man."

Sounds like a line from a John Wayne movie or rather from a Wayne movie genre that was just beginning to evolve at Warners back in 1933. Much later in films like *McLintock!* (1963), Wayne tried to clean up his act by rescuing a redskin literally from the hangman's noose, and standing off an angry crowd with the full force of a quietly delivered, "I speak for the Comanche." But it appears to have done him little good as Indian activists, loath to relinquish such a highly visible target, branded such scenes as maudlin (which they were) and insincere, which may be too strong a word for ineptly expressed good intentions.

*A character role for Lone Star Productions in 1934. He plays
a government undercover agent in RAINBOW VALLEY.*

"Them fight scenes were sure somethin'." — *George "Gabby" Hayes*

6.
SINGIN' SANDY SAUNDERS

The motion picture saloon-style, table-shattering, bar-toppling, chair-smashing brawl as we know it today owes a great deal to John Wayne. We tend to take those punches that send the recipient hurtling through a plate glass window for granted. Transpose the action from the wild west to World War Two, and the scenario is still the same: Wayne takes a couple of good licks from his opponent then proceeds to demolish him.

During the silent era, it was enough to see motion on the screen. Punches that palpably didn't land, villains dropping at the merest flick of the hero's fist, the protagonist dispatching a roomful of baddies without sustaining a smudge or a bruise, all were commonplace on the silent screen. The need for character delineation without sound called for the broadest interpretations. The hero, assuming a Marquis of Queensberry stance, had chairs, bottles and tables broken over his noble head until, tiring of the game, he downed his nefarious opponent with a deft one-two, neither of which, the viewer could clearly see, landed.

When Wayne moved from Warners to Lone Star Productions, an independent sprouting from Poverty Row's Monogram, he took with him the beginning of a kind of repertory company, in George Hayes (who would become a screen fixture as the bearded, irrepressible sourdough Gabby Hayes, gumming his way through countless westerns) and Yakima Canutt. Wayne was committed to sixteen films budgeted at ten thousand dollars each, and filmed in three-and-a-half days. That kind of schedule, filming virtually the same plot with only cast and locale changes, can be very wearing on even the most seasoned actor, which at the time Duke was not.

Every picture, with interchangeable titles like *Blue Steel*, *The Dawn Rider*, and *Riders of Destiny*, had to have a big brawl with Wayne getting hit from all angles by countless break-away balsa-wood tables, chairs, and fake bottles. Even the specially constructed props—made to disintegrate spectacularly on contact—can become irritating when delivered in quantity. The story has it that Wayne, frustrated at the fists-only screen hero code, in the middle of a fight scene suddenly picked up a chair and brained an astonished attacker. "Why," he is said to have demanded, while director Robert North Bradbury (cowboy star Bob Steele's father) screamed "Cut!" "can't the hero give as good as he gets?" We can almost see him standing there waiting for an answer.

Canutt was frequently involved in the violent action, either as Wayne's double or as the principal bad guy. The two actors began working out little fight routines, choreographing their punches, and someone suggested filming over each combatant's shoulder so the punches would appear to land. The fights suddenly took on a new realism that caused the Lone Star quickies to get more attention than perhaps they merited.

Lone Star was responsible for another milestone, John

Wayne's first and last appearance as Singin' Sandy Saunders, hero of *Riders of Destiny*. Wayne plays a government man working undercover, sent to help some ranchers whose land is being taken over by an unscrupulous speculator. If you can imagine a typical John Wayne walk down the main street only to have him inexplicably break out into song in a voice that doesn't match his own (in this case a singer named Smith Ballew), you get some idea of the scene's impact. The star's survival instinct, the awareness of what was right for him, quickly terminated the singing-cowboy idea, especially when he was asked to warble some current favorites for spectators during personal appearances.

In *West of the Divide*, the fourth in the Lone Star series, we hear the beginnings of the speech pattern learned from Canutt and honed to perfection as Wayne gained experience. One line, "I've seen that fella somewhere . . . but I can't think when," has him make the deliberate off-beat hesitations he described earlier in these pages. ". . . But I can't think when," is transformed from a near throwaway line into a suspense-inducing promise of a future confrontation. Once his character, Ted Hayden, does remember when, the reading clearly tells us, watch out!

It is easy now to see the pattern of the star's gradual emergence as a screen personality, but his success must be viewed in the context of scores of other serial and "B" picture leads' failure to survive. An ingenue named Phyllis Isley came up the same hard trail to eventually become Jennifer Jones; Marsha Hunt and George Brent also served the long serials-to-"B"-to-star apprenticeship, but they were the exceptions rather than the rule.

Allen Eyles notes that not only Wayne's talk but his walk began taking on a definite cadence during this 1933 to 1935 period. Reviewing *Randy Rides Alone* Eyles observes: "Wayne's walk in this film has a lazy air of increasing confidence, and he is seen twirling his six-shooter with professional ease . . ." Clearly the big man is beginning to believe that he is the embodiment of the classic western hero, and his growing self-assurance shows up on the screen.

He had not yet, however, reached the stage of professional objectivity that would permit him to poke fun at himself later in his career. "I'll be damned if I'm not the stuff men are made of," he commented after reading favorable reviews on his macho image in

Hondo (1953). And that, about as well as anything, sums up the fans' perception of the man who was listed among motion picture box-offices' top ten in drawing power for twenty straight years, a feat roughly comparable to a .500 hitter in baseball or a thoroughbred winning the Triple Crown in three successive seasons.

A list of the top ten most-watched television shows in the medium's history includes the 1970 Academy Awards when Wayne won his Oscar for *True Grit*, a statistic that seems more than coincidental to the millions of eager viewers who felt that the star should have gotten that award long ago just for being himself. Which, of course, is why he finally won, as he acknowledged by describing his portrayal of Reuben J. "Rooster" Cogburn as that of a "mean, cantankerous, old son-of-a-bitch, just like me." His brief, tearful acceptance speech at Los Angeles's Dorothy Chandler Pavilion produced the now classic line, "If I'd known what I know now, I'd have put a patch on my eye thirty-five years ago."

"Duke is the marrying kind."
— Ward Bond

7.
ENTER JOSIE

In 1933 John Wayne, beginning to see the glimmerings of his own image, married Josephine Saenz, the daughter of a Panamanian diplomat. The first Mrs. Wayne was soon busy producing babies, keeping track of her husband, and adjusting to being married to a man who had the star bit in his teeth. Four children, Michael in 1934, Toni in 1935, Patrick in 1938, and Melinda in 1940, could not provide a family stability to match the demanding schedule that followed *Stagecoach* in 1939. The couple were separated in 1942, but not before Duke had his first sampling of the fertile minds of the Hollywood studio press agents.

With his marriage in trouble because of long working hours, and a penchant for relaxing over some firewater with a growing "stock company" that included Yak Canutt, a U.S.C. ex-medical student named Wardell Bond, and Victor McLaglen, an image-protecting article titled *Mother Wayne* appeared magically in the October, 1940 issue of *Photoplay*. Writer Sally Reid described the

Wayne household as an oasis of domestic tranquility, assuring her eager readers that their Hollywood neighbors had nicknamed them "The Bumsteads" after the comic strip, and that Josie and Duke were known to intimates as "Dagwood" and "Blondie," and their children as "the baby Dumplings."

Another fan piece, after confiding that Wayne had really wanted to become a lawyer, reported that, "He cried at sad movies, or when someone played *Liebestraum* on the accordion." A killing work schedule, a driving ambition to succeed, and a natural affinity for male and female companionship, combined to make his first as well as two succeeding marriages finally fail.

Wayne was given a second chance to jump another "B" picture hurdle in 1935 when Lone Star and Mascot joined to form Republic Pictures, and signed him to star in their very first production, *Westward Ho!* While still a "B" western, *Westward Ho!* was budgeted at nearly forty thousand dollars and was intended as a showcase of the new studio's superior product featuring larger casts and more location footage. The picture and the seven that followed between 1935 and 1936 were more elaborately mounted than their predecessors, but were still in the "B" category when Duke signed with Universal, his second major studio, in the latter part of 1936. He sings his last screen song in *Westward Ho!*, a dubbed ditty which he warbles to heroine Sheila Manners before riding out to gun down villain Yakima Canutt.

Universal's sixty to seventy thousand dollar budget gave Wayne a chance at better stories, more wardrobe, stronger supporting casts, and, most importantly, at being reviewed in newspapers as the bottom half of a first-run double bill. He was cast in *Conflict*, based on Jack London's story *The Abysmal Brute*, first released as a 1923 silent starring Reginald Denny, as a mining-town brawler who develops enough of a reputation with his fists to take on touring prizefighter Ward Bond (who would continue to be called Wardell by Wayne throughout their long, close friendship).

Wayne has a chance to get all duded up in this picture and is cast as a sneaky type secretly in cahoots with Bond to throw the fight. Even though he eventually sees the light, and comes through for pretty reporter Jean Rogers, it is not the kind of role he would permit himself later in his career. The sense of what was

The star of newly formed Republic Pictures' first film,
WESTWARD HO!, in 1936. And the beginning of an important
relationship with stunt man Yakima Canutt.

The Duke all duded up for CONFLICT, his first with
Universal at the end of 1936.

With Jean Rogers and Ward Bond. His role in CONFLICT was not in keeping with his later image.

right for himself that he developed after *Stagecoach*, and was in a position to enforce as he became a big box-office attraction, was very clear in his mind.

"I always look for a story with basic emotions," Wayne explains. "A dog, a kid, a woman's love, a man's love." Then he molds his screen personality close to the advice he gave his own sons. Keep your word at all costs; be courteous, even when provoked; and don't ever start a fight, but if one gets started—finish it.

When it was suggested that his screen roles emphasize a reliance on violence as a solution to many of life's problems, the star protested, "I'm not a combative-type guy. I'm a smiling-type guy."

Yet clearly the real life Wayne, like the screen counterpart, believes in drawing a line that can be crossed only at the intruder's

With Louise Latimer in CALIFORNIA STRAIGHT AHEAD in 1937.
The title may have been deliberately misleading.

peril. When asked by writer Pete Martin about alleged barroom altercations, Duke, choosing his words carefully, replied in a 1950 *Saturday Evening Post* interview: "Frequently I have to let my hair grow long for a picture. This leads to strangers I meet suggesting that I have characteristics usually associated with long hair, that are foreign to my nature. I resent these insinuations."

Now if that isn't a John Wayne speech directed to the screen heavy just prior to the roof falling in, I don't know one.

California Straight Ahead, his next for Republic, again keeps him out of the saddle (although the title may have been intentionally misleading for his large number of cowboy fans) and finds him driving a truck at the head of a caravan racing the

Showing increasing versatility, he plays a hockey star in
IDOL OF THE CROWDS (1937) here being comforted by Sheila Bromley.

railroad across the continent, and finally winning despite every imaginable natural obstacle.

In *I Cover the War* Wayne plays a newsreel cameraman and in *Idol of the Crowds* he returns to a more familiar physical role as a hockey star who lets it all hang out in the final game, an ice version of the barroom brawl and shoot-out. His last for Republic during that period, *Adventure's End*, has him as a pearl diver, and completes an unusual, for him, five-picture series without a western story. Almost as if he sensed the possible error of his shift away from the western, he made one picture for Paramount during that period, *Born to the West* in which his female interest was another fugitive from the ten thousand dollar quickie, Marsha Hunt, and which showed the audience a first fleeting glimpse of a bit player named Alan Ladd.

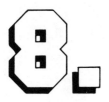

8.

THE THREE MESQUITEERS

Then came a western series starring a trio whose name sounds like a Saturday morning children's television cartoon show, *The Three Mesquiteers*. Alexandre Dumas may not have approved (or understood) but the 1930s and '40s movie-going public took the three swash-, or sagebucklers to their hearts. Wayne, as head Mesquiteer Stony Brooke appeared in eight of the series before *Stagecoach* beckoned him to stardom in 1939. He turned his role over to actor Bob Livingston, and rode off into his last "B" picture sunset.

But with *Stagecoach* not yet on the horizon, being partnered with fellow Mesquiteers Max Terhune and Ray Corrigan enabled him to gain valuable acting experience. Despite the fact that Wayne's Stony Brooke was only one of three leads, he always emerged as the first among equals, and was the character around

*PALS OF THE SADDLE (1938). His first as one of The
Three Mesquiteers with Max Terhune (center) and
Ray Corrigan, gave him valuable acting experience.*

whom most of the action evolved. The other two, Terhune's Lullaby and Corrigan's Tucson, acted as the scriptwriters' *deus ex machina* as they hovered in the background available to come to their partner's, and the plot's, rescue.

Despite their "B" category the pictures integrated up-to-date plots into familiar western surroundings giving Wayne an opportunity to combine his ease in the saddle with situations that non-western fans could accept. *Pals of the Saddle*, for example, had the security of the United States as its central theme. Some bad guys were manufacturing a lethal gas using a chemical found only in the western badlands. They would smuggle the raw material across the border into Mexico where the gas was manufactured.

Without going into plot intricacies, Wayne befriends a female government agent played by Doreen McKay whose job is to track down the evil group. When some male agents working with her are slain, Wayne steps in, in the nick of time cuts off a wagon train transporting the deadly cargo and personally disposes of the lead bad guy. But not before Lullaby and Tucson have rescued *him* from captivity enabling him to go for the big finish.

It's difficult for us to grasp that future stars like Marsha Hunt, Alan Ladd, and Jennifer Jones made their first tentative screen appearances in motion pictures in which John Wayne was even then the featured player, if not the star. *The Three Mesquiteers* series was no exception. In *Three Texas Steers* our trio set out to save the ranch of circus owner Nancy Evans. She has inherited both ranch and circus, but is in danger of losing the former to some unscrupulous louts who want to dam up the water supply, and run out all the small ranchers. The heavies try to get to Nancy by causing accidents at her circus. Wayne and the other two

Raymond Hatton replaced Mesquiteer Max Terhune (with Wayne and Corrigan) in THREE TEXAS STEERS, a 1939 film that introduced ingenue Carole Landis.

Poised on the brink of stardom. He has just completed FRONTIER HORIZON, his last Mesquiteer picture before STAGECOACH. This 1939 film introduced young actress Phyllis Isley, later known as Jennifer Jones.

finally foil the bad men saving the circus and ranch for their heroine, played by ingenue Carole Landis.

Despite horses and assorted wild animals running amok and stealing scenes, the Duke more than acquits himself as the stand-out good guy. Later in his career, in 1964, he would be involved in another picture *Circus World* (also released as *The Magnificent Showman*) co-starring John Smith, Claudia Cardinale, and Rita Hayworth. Both pictures featured a fire in the big top which gave the big man a chance to get in some action heroics. The films have one other thing in common: Despite a several million dollar budget difference, they were both probably viewed by approximately the same number of people. One reason for the second picture's poor showing—that reveals an interesting side of Wayne's private personality—will be discussed later in this chronology.

Frontier Horizon, the last Mesquiteer picture made before Duke went with John Ford to do *Stagecoach*, is remembered principally because the leading lady, Celia, was played by the aforementioned Phyllis Isley.

*As The Ringo Kid, the role that jumped him to stardom in
STAGECOACH directed by John Ford in 1939.*

"Chrissakes—stop slurring your lines, you dumb bastard." —John Ford

STAGECOACH

Most Hollywood personalities achieve stardom gradually. In the days of the major-studio contract "stables," men and women were carefully groomed through a succession of minor roles to finally take over screen center, and be billed as top stars. A few performers, however, achieved stardom in a single, instantly recallable picture. He or she may not have commanded immediate fame or big money as a result of one role but, looking back, it can be generally agreed that a specific picture stamped "Star" across the player's billing from that time on.

Alan Ladd in *This Gun For Hire*, and Humphrey Bogart in *The Petrified Forest*, are two outstanding examples; a third is John Wayne in *Stagecoach*. Much has been written about director John Ford's struggle to get the screenplay based on Ernest Haycox's short story *Stage To Lordsburg* financed and produced, as well as how the director had Wayne in mind for the part for several years before finally getting Walter Wanger to put the deal together.

What is perhaps not generally understood is that Ford was taking a big risk casting the relatively unproven actor, not just with the picture but with his own career. Ford had not made a western since *Three Bad Men* in 1926, and he needed a big box-office success. Actually Wayne was worse than a little-known actor, he was a known actor: A certified "B" picture lead who had bombed out in *The Big Trail*. Bankers who financed pictures, especially big budget westerns, a largely untested category, had long memories, and Ford had some difficult times until Wanger agreed to produce the picture. Even then it was decreed that Claire Trevor's name would appear first on the credits as box-office insurance. Wayne was paid a total of six thousand dollars for his work.

In retrospect the plot seemed to have very little going for it; a group of people, a boozy doctor (Thomas Mitchell, who won an Academy Award for the portrayal), a gambler (John Carradine), a lady of easy virtue (Claire Trevor), a real lady (Louise Platt), and a whiskey salesman (Donald Meek) are headed west in an overland stage driven by Andy Devine with George Bancroft riding shotgun. The stage is stopped by a lone man on foot whose horse has gone lame. The scene where John Wayne as the Ringo Kid, saddle in one hand, Winchester in the other, fires a round in the air to halt the reluctant Devine, seemed literally to be what the big man had been waiting for all those years.

Under Ford's persistent, apparently at times cruelly critical direction, Wayne fought with the part and stayed in character so successfully that he appeared transformed as an actor. Lazy habits, the walk, the speech pattern, the overwhelming size that had gotten him through so many forgettable pictures, now had themselves to be, if not forgotten, at least subjugated to the main business of playing a role. By all accounts it was not easy, partly because Wayne had come to at least partially believe that either he would make it on presence alone or not at all. He was unwilling to experiment with anything beyond the most basic reactions. "I don't act, I react," he told an interviewer at the time.

Ford realized that the talent surrounding his young actor could either play off him or completely bury him; the director gambled that by goading Wayne mercilessly, he would bring out the spark he was certain existed, and by so doing give Wayne's

*Seated beside Andy Devine on the stagecoach while
George Bancroft (left) reassures a townsman.*

natural intelligence and acting instincts full rein for the first time.

It worked, but not without help from a particularly sensitive script by Dudley Nichols, and some timely planning and stunt work by, yes, Yakima Canutt. Canutt helped stage some of the most memorable fight scenes between Bancroft from the driver's seat, Wayne sitting atop the stage, and a band of mounted Apaches, ever filmed. Ford's use of Monument Valley in Arizona for the exteriors, and the matching studio close shots filmed in front of a rear-projection screen, have rarely if ever been equaled as a sustained long-range study of a thrilling, running fight, and the close, individual reactions of the participants.

One of those individual reactions involved another unforgettable scene that did much to establish Wayne as a fearless leading man. The driver Buck (Andy Devine) yells a warning as a hard-riding Indian overtakes the wagon and jumps on the lead horses. Wayne whirls, fires, and hits the Indian (adding to his later Indian movement troubles) just as Buck is wounded in the arm and drops the long reins. Unhesitatingly, Wayne leaps past the slumping driver, jumps down on the slim, wooden singletrees bucking and swaying between the hard-running horses, leaps ahead to the middle team, then jumps again to the leading pair of horses to retrieve the loose reins and keep the stage ahead of the howling Apaches. Canutt doubled for Wayne on that stunt, once more contributing substantially to the future star's reputation as a screen daredevil.

Wayne pretty much signals his approach to tender love scenes when, part way through the picture, he declares his intentions to Claire Trevor's Dallas, a fallen woman who has achieved new self-respect through his insistence on treating her as a lady.

"You got no folks," the Ringo Kid drawls. "Neither have I. (pause) I got a ranch across the border, (pause) there's a river and trees. (pause) A man could live there (pause) and a woman. (*long* pause) Will you go?"

Dallas, stunned by his impassioned plea, flees in confusion. It's all right, though, they get together in the end. The charm of their first encounter has to do with Dallas understanding that he doesn't know about her background, and our believing that he doesn't know! There lies the strength and, if you will, the magic of

John Wayne as we know him today. He championed the cause of the most obvious whore-with-a-heart-of-gold ever to appear on the screen, and actually believed she was straight. And because the Ringo Kid thought she was a lady, she began to acquire self-respect and we, the audience, believed in her as well.

Wayne does that again and again in later pictures, practically defying us not to believe in his character and usually winning us over. There are those, however, he did not win over and that minority can be very vocal, indeed.

Critic John Simon, a master of snide sophistry, writes, ". . . the Duke could perhaps be defined as a cross between a face on Mount Rushmore and a head on Easter Island atop a doric column that moves with a swagger, talks in a monotone to which a drawl adds a slight curlicue, and looks at you with a lazy gaze that starts out downward but then curves slowly upward. Every era gets that leader it deserves; John Wayne is ours."

Curlicue aside, New Yorker Simon reflects a segment of the viewing public's antipathy toward Wayne's professional and private image: They resent the idea that the actor seems essentially to be playing himself on screen with all the macho, violence-oriented, gut values implied.

However with critics, as with lawyers and politicians, someone of equal or greater stature is always available to espouse the opposite view, in this case respected movie reviewer Molly Haskell.

"For as long as I can remember," Ms. Haskell writes, "John Wayne has been abused by the Eastern Intelligentsia and judged more for his politics than his performances. Critics who blithely ignore the macho swagger and emphasis on he-man athleticism in the roles a chic liberal like Paul Newman plays, leap on Wayne as the Godzilla of American Imperialism."

A review of *Stagecoach* by the *New Yorker* magazine's John McCarten contributed to Wayne's long disenchantment with the eastern press establishment. After mentioning the cinematographers, the still photographer, and director Ford, the review concludes with, "The actors and actresses are mostly familiar persons, like Claire Trevor, and some genuine Apaches, so we are told, have bolted out of the reservation to contribute their little bit toward the progress of art." No other actor was mentioned.

Wayne, a regular *New Yorker* reader, never forgot that deliberate, juvenile slight.

We'll have more to say here about our subject and his alleged and actual views on politics; at this point it suffices to note that *Stagecoach* launched a career that now seems to have been inevitable but was far from being preordained at the time.

The look that, for many, typifies America, is born. A poll would show that only Abraham Lincoln's face was better known.

"I must say that Duke sits a horse well." — *George Sanders*

10.

FROM B TO A

Wayne's personal life appeared to be going as well as his public one during the *Stagecoach* period. Patrick had been born the year before and Melinda would make her appearance the next year, signifying some kind of marital harmony. But appearances were deceiving, and it would be only two years later, in 1942, that the Waynes would separate, with a final divorce decree granted in 1945.

The jump from "B" to "A" picture status, from also-ran to star, involved the actor in a taxing professional and social life. He moved from one picture to the next, sometimes with only a few days' rest, working long hours, and relaxing with equal intensity. Making pictures was no longer a walk-through, a chase, some dialogue, and a final brawl. Studios began spending hundreds of thousands of dollars on his pictures and casting him with people whose acting talents made greater demands on his own.

Ward Bond was now a frequent on- and off-screen companion, and it can be assumed—Wayne himself would never discuss it—

that his career and his delight in hoisting a couple with Bond, character actor Grant Withers and Canutt at the end of a hard day's work was incompatible with a structured family life.

And work there was aplenty although not always as financially or professionally rewarding as Wayne would have liked. His contract with Republic allowed him a greater freedom than he would have had if the studio executives could have anticipated *Stagecoach*. Not being able to tie the newly-rising star to themselves exclusively, these practical-minded men did the next best thing, they tapped into his newfound popularity by casting him in a half-million-dollar big budget picture with a good script, and a strong supporting cast. The result was *The Dark Command* pairing him once again with Claire Trevor, directed by Raoul Walsh, and co-starring Walter Pidgeon borrowed from MGM to give the epic some class.

The Dark Command had to wait because Wayne had already made a deal with RKO Radio Pictures who pulled a favorite Hollywood trick by capitalizing on another studio's thunder and, with something less than brilliance, exploiting the Trevor-Wayne combination. *Allegheny Uprising*, a prerevolutionary story, features Wayne as an American patriot before there was a United States of America, and pits him against military commander Captain Swanson, played by George Sanders. Brian Donlevy as Callender, who sells contraband to the Indians under protection of a crown license, and Claire Trevor as a ballsy frontier girl enamored of Wayne, complete the strong cast. The picture never really got off the ground despite good production values, and Wayne was happy to see it and 1939 behind him as he looked forward to keeping his *Stagecoach* momentum going.

Reunited with Walsh for the first time since *The Big Trail* disaster, Wayne brought a new maturity and sureness to his role in *The Dark Command*. Most interestingly, more by accident than design, this picture marks Wayne's first identification with what would today be called the conservative, no-nonsense approach to questions of law and order, as well as related political philosophies. Wayne's character runs for sheriff against the more polished Walter Pidgeon's Will Cantrell (based on the real-life Charles Quantrill).

Pidgeon is concerned with right and wrong as moral abstrac-

"B" pictures forever behind him, he shows a new self-assurance in
THE DARK COMMAND, made the year after STAGECOACH.

tions while Wayne campaigns on the simplistic bad-guys-against-the-good-guys platform. The 1940 version of liberal versus conservative ends up with Wayne being elected, and becoming a conscientious sheriff. Cantrell, embittered by his defeat, begins forming a band of roughnecks who will eventually be known to real-life history as Quantrill's Raiders. In the picture a sub-plot has Wayne falling in love with town beauty Claire Trevor, and a final confrontation in which Wayne guns down a now thoroughly discredited Cantrell.

Once again the ubiquitous Yakima Canutt hovered in the background, this time as second unit director, and was responsible for the staging of one particularly spectacular escape scene, and doubling for the star as well. This picture might be described as the transition between fade-out the Canutt era and fade-in the Wayne legend; from now on the actor would leave the simpler screen life behind and begin to enjoy, and contend with, the larger-than-life on- and off-screen image that followed his new-found fame.

"John Wayne needs no protection from me." — *Cecil B. DeMille*

11.

THE DUKE
AND DIETRICH

Three Faces West, Wayne's next picture, accomplished two things: It reinforced his stubbornness-to-change, self-reliant screen personality, and considerably broadened the demands on him as an actor. His mentor John Ford had just made *The Grapes of Wrath*, starring Henry Fonda, a classic study of the hardships imposed on middle-western farmers by the prolonged drought in what became known as the Dust Bowl. Duke finds himself in the same Dust Bowl championing farmers' rights, but unlike Fonda, reluctant to face the realities of a desperate situation. He wants to stand and fight; the dust, the poverty, and what he perceives as men's weakness in the face of adversity.

After drowning his manly sorrows in a saloon (giving rise in this and subsequent pictures to critics' charges that getting drunk and knocking someone down summed up the actor's professional and private solution to almost any problem), Wayne decides to organize a trek to Oregon. When a farmer protests that, "We can always stay here and go on relief," Wayne replies witheringly, "That's right, (pause) you can," marking the man as a low-life shirker as far as the theater audience is concerned.

Which brings up a point. Henry L. Mencken once said, "No one will ever go broke underestimating the intelligence of the American public," an observation that present-day television shows are making dismayingly valid. In contrast the 1940s' writers, directors, and producers knew what the audience wanted: Hard work and ethical values, simply expressed; John Wayne happened to be able to get that message across better than anyone around. Sure, he means many of the lines he says on the screen, but that doesn't mean that he should be singled out as some kind of a bareknuckled zombie incapable of grasping subtleties in behavior or philosophy.

In his next picture, *The Long Voyage Home*, he left the security of the open range because he trusted John Ford who directed the film, based on four of Eugene O'Neill's one-act plays. Walter Wanger, whose *Stagecoach* gamble paid off, was ready to finance another leap forward in Duke's career. Surrounded by a fine supporting cast that includes Thomas Mitchell, Ian Hunter, Barry Fitzgerald, Mildred Natwick, Ward Bond and Arthur Shields, Wayne jumps unhesitatingly into the role of sailor Ole Olsen, Swedish accent and all.

Ole is a simple man of good heart who possesses great physical strength, and an unshakable set of personal values. Like the Ringo Kid he befriends a whore, here played by—are you ready—Mildred Natwick, and addresses her courteously right up to the moment he passes out from knockout drops she has slipped into his drink. About to be shanghaied, he is rescued by his shipmates and put aboard a ship bound for his native Sweden.

It's been a long voyage for Ole partly because, until his final rescue, every time he saves up enough money to quit the sea, he good-naturedly goes ashore with his buddies, gets drunk, and loses his poke.

Although there's not a horse in sight, Ole is an even more simplified version of the trusting, drinking, honorable character

*THE LONG VOYAGE HOME (1940) gave him a challenging
role that featured his first screen accent.*

In SEVEN SINNERS (1940) Marlene Dietrich falls in love with Duke but selflessly steps out of his life. Off camera the ending was different.

*Things were tough all over during REAP THE WILD WIND in 1942. Killed
by a giant squid in the picture (his first screen death), in real
life he was separated from first wife Josephine Saenz Morrison.*

Showing a broadening acting range in PITTSBURGH (1942) as coal miner
turned successful businessman, he is fitted here for his
new image by Shemp Howard better known as one of
The Three Stooges, appearing in a rare straight dramatic role.

the movie-goer had come to know and love.

Duke stayed with the sea in *Seven Sinners*, and stayed right in character as the chivalrous, ingenuous he-man Navy lieutenant who hears sultry nightclub singer Marlene Dietrich perform in the Seven Sinners Cafe. That's as close as you'll come to sin in this unpretentious film that features a great sequence in which Dietrich is singing *The Man's in the Navy*, (See those shoulders, broad and glorious . . .) as Wayne enters the cafe looking very broad and glorious in his dress whites. The camera cutting from one to the other to punctuate the lyrics, establishes both characters in an unusually eloquent dialogue-free scene.

Dietrich falls in love with Wayne but realizes that she will be harmful to his career. When the plot has him knocked out at the end of a well-staged barroom brawl, she seizes the opportunity to slip away, leaving him untainted by her past in his clean-cut, all-American pursuit of a military career.

In real life it may have been a different story. An off-screen friendship developed between Duke and Dietrich that probably contributed to the breakup of his first marriage, and was most certainly involved in his second. Wife number two, Esperanza Baur, mentioned the blond star in an acrimonious divorce action fully thirteen years later, in 1953, confirming both Wayne's at-

Randolph Scott listens as "Pittsburgh" Markham talks about Josie, co-star Marlene Dietrich's character, in a conversation that had a meaning lost on the movie audience.

Another PITTSBURGH costume change that shows the interesting development of his screen portrayal.

tachment to old friends and Dietrich's staying power.

Leading ladies aside, Duke's home life was deteriorating. Josie Morrison (she refused to call herself Mrs. Wayne) was a society lady and a strong Roman Catholic. Her friends included Loretta Young and Irene Dunne, leaders of the socially prominent Hollywood Catholic community. Mrs. Morrison liked to give formal dinners, poetry readings, and other white-tie affairs, and expected Mr. Morrison to attend. Mr. Morrison, working long hours and under considerable professional pressure, was apt to arrive home tired, wanting only to wrap his large fist around a tumbler full of bourbon, and relax. A cocktail before dinner, and one or two sips of wine with the main course, were not his cup of booze.

Often he would come home to find several priests and nuns in attendance. He began preparing for these confrontations by having a few belts after work. His manner, by his own admission, tended to become somewhat coarse and outspoken when he was thrust into situations that made him uneasy, especially when he had fortified himself with firewater for the occasion. By all accounts Wayne is one of those people who can drink substantial quantities of alcohol on a regular basis over a forty-year period, and not damage himself either physically or emotionally.

Almost anyone who has worked with him for any length of time has a favorite story of Duke on location, watching half the cast and crew fall by the wayside in the small hours of the morning in some local bar, leaving him in solitary splendor, loaded but upright. And next morning, he would be the only one reporting for work on time, makeup on, in costume, and knowing his lines while lesser (and younger) actors nursed massive hangovers.

But while he was drinking he could be coarse and combative, neither condition being acceptable to Josie Saenz Morrison. So, despite his declared love for her and his concern for the four children, they separated about the time *Seven Sinners* and *Reap The Wild Wind*, the latter co-starring Ray Milland and Paulette Goddard, were made. He was in big company in *Reap The Wild Wind*, the only picture he made with Cecil B. DeMille. Besides Milland (who had top billing) and Goddard, the cast included Raymond Massey, Robert Preston, and Susan Hayward. The negotiations leading to Wayne accepting the role tell us a great

*He played a pharmacist, his late father's profession, opposite
Helen Parrish in IN OLD CALIFORNIA (1942).*

deal about his professional awareness. He was on loan from Republic going into a Paramount picture, with a Paramount producer, and Milland, a Paramount star.

Duke had a private meeting with DeMille during which he expressed his fear that Milland would naturally be given camera preference and that he, Wayne, would have no one to "protect" him from getting the worse of the key scenes. Here was one thorough professional dealing with another, and DeMille respected him; the producer-director gave Wayne his word that he wouldn't be made to look bad and the actor never had cause to regret taking the role.

A giant squid accomplished what countless Apaches failed to do: Kill John Wayne. His first screen death is heroic as he saves Milland's life at the cost of his own.

Wayne made two more pictures with Dietrich in 1942, *The Spoilers* and *Pittsburgh*, both co-starring Randolph Scott. By now Wayne had moved out of his home, and was spending a great deal of time with Marlene, often visiting for long evenings at her house "watching a whole bunch of movies" as he told an acquaintance at the time. In one of those coincidences that Duke obviously chose not to avoid, La Dietrich's character in *Pittsburgh*, a coal miner's daughter of easy morals, is named Josie, a circumstance certainly not lost on Mrs. Morrison or her high-toned Hollywood friends.

Wayne and Scott proved to be a good working team on both pictures. Although Scott got top billing, Wayne had the meatier roles and made the most of them. Duke was about as far away from the saddle as he could get, appearing as a gold miner in *The Spoilers* and as Pittsburgh Markham ("a big name for a big man"), a coal miner with ambitions in the second film. *The Spoilers* features an energetic fight scene that was becoming his trademark, but it is *Pittsburgh* that interests us more as Wayne-watchers. In it Wayne self-servingly marries a banker's daughter, finds himself ill at ease at the wedding reception, and seeks solace with the earthy Josie on his wedding night! The ironic analogy to his personal life at that time is inescapable.

Duke may not have liked the real-life Josie's white-tie affairs, but in his role as a successful businessman in the picture, he wears formal clothes with the naturalness and ease of an ac-

FLYING TIGERS, made in busy 1942, was the first of a long string of patriotic war films. Here co-starring Anna Lee and Paul Kelly.

complished actor. His character progression from humble miner to ruthless exploiter of people to a final awareness of finer human values is a dress rehearsal for the powerful part of Thomas Dunson he would play six years later in *Red River*.

About the only thing of interest to us in Republic's *In Old California* starring Wayne in that very busy 1942 is his portrayal of Tom Craig, a young Boston pharmacist come West to Sacramento to set himself up in business, and who is attracted to nice girl Helen Parrish. Some fan magazine writers (undoubtedly nudged by studio flacks) made a big deal out of the star's strong emotions at getting a chance to represent his late father's profession on the screen. The idea of casting John Wayne as a pharma-cist, of all things, is just far enough out to suggest that he may have had a more than passing interest in playing the part.

Pharmacist Craig manages to end up leading a wagon train through a blockade to deliver much-needed drugs to epidemic-struck mines, providing some action insurance for an otherwise pedestrian plot.

Flying Tigers, another 1942 Wayne starrer (no wonder the man needed a taste at the end of the day!) has him cast in the role originated by Cary Grant in Howard Hawks's *Only Angels Have Wings* with the locale changed from South America to China. Wayne, with Anna Lee and Paul Kelly in supporting roles, heads some fliers fighting the Japanese prior to Pearl Harbor. John Carroll co-stars as a devil-may-care flyboy who turns patriotic when the Japs strike Pearl. This is Duke's first patriotic war film, and he does as well as can be expected sitting in a dummy fighter-plane cockpit on a sound stage grimly firing deadly bursts into the savage, inept enemy. An interesting sidelight is Carroll's opportunity to climb a step up the "B" ladder to "A" picture stardom; despite one of the best acting roles of his career he never quite made it; the Hollywood competition was fierce and many competent, photogenic actors and actresses fell by the wayside on the difficult march toward success.

An unusual photograph taken on location with THE FIGHTING
SEABEES (1944) in that the star is not immediately recognizable
and is in civilian clothes surrounded by uniforms.

"I always thought I was a liberal."
—*J.W.*

12.
COMMUNISM IN HOLLYWOOD

John Wayne gave his life for the cause in *The Fighting Seabees* in 1944, the second time his screen character died. Both were heroic deaths, saving Ray Milland's life in *Reap The Wild Wind*, and saving vital Pacific fleet oil supplies from "Tojo and his bug-eyed monkeys." Although Pearl Harbor occurred during *The Flying Tigers*, this picture, dedicated to the famous Army (C.B.) Construction Battalions, is the first full-scale morale-boosting film in a series that had the star fighting the Japs instead of western bad men and, of course, the Indians.

Wayne is Wedge Donovan, the civilian boss of a construction crew organized to build front-line installations on the heels of advancing combat troops. Despite the picture's limited production values—it was mostly special effects and rear projection screens—he manages to get across a good characterization of a man driven to action at the sight of his defenseless workers being picked off by Japanese snipers. He finally arms his men, and leads a foolhardy attack that costs many lives and foils an army ambush plan. Once again anticipating his role in *Red River* he admits that "I was wrong, rotten, wrong," (even as Walter Brennan would tell Thomas Dunson "You wuz wrong, Mr. Dunson. Dead wrong.") and makes amends by sacrificing himself to destroy a Jap raiding party and save the precious oil.

Critics who saw Wayne's parts as lacking depth simply failed, or refused, to acknowledge his steady growth as an actor ready to accept the challenge of roles such as those in *Reap The Wild Wind*, *Pittsburgh*, and *The Fighting Seabees*. These portrayals show him in an unsympathetic light, then shade his character so that we are looking at a different man at picture's end. That's what writing and acting are all about. When critic Stanley Kauffman writes about ". . . the Wayne career of almost forty years in which, give or take the minor characteristic here and there and changes of costume, the star has altered only by very slowly growing older," one must conclude either that the writer has not seen Wayne's earlier films, or that he is simply following what he takes to be the currently popular critical line.

1945 was a memorable year for John Wayne on both a personal and professional level. His divorce from Mrs. Josephine Saenz Morrison became final; he had met, and was planning to marry Mexican actress Esperanza Baur Diaz Ceballos who would, through seven tempestuous years, be known as his beloved Chata (Spanish for pugnose); his feelings against those he deemed disloyal to his country would deepen; and he would make an outstanding war picture that features one of his better performances.

The divorce was inevitable and, considering that Josie pretty well cleaned him out financially, harmonious. He acknowledged that they were simply two different people with temperaments that grew further apart as he became more successful, and she was forced into the role of a Hollywood wife, painted on the backdrop of scenes from his public life. But she was a good mother and he a good father; it is a tribute to them both that their four children grew up without the emotional traumas that seem so much a part of show-business children whose parents have split up.

Esperanza was another matter; there was nothing inevitable

There was real life off-screen drama during the filming of
BACK TO BATAAN *(here with Paul Fix) in 1945 as Duke*
confronted some film industry Communists.

about her. She was married when Wayne first met her in Mexico
City, a very sensual woman both in appearance and projection.
Duke, drawn again to a Latin type, was mightily smitten; after an
initial separation when he returned to Hollywood, they were
reunited and married three weeks after his divorce became final,
on January 18, 1946. As we shall see, Duke, Chata, and Chata's
mother did not live happily then or ever after.

The star's growing disillusionment with communist sym-
pathizers was partly a result of his experience on *Back to Bataan*,
one of a series of avowedly patriotic films he made during that
period. A group of Hollywood creative people had, in 1944,

formed the Motion Picture Alliance for the Preservation of American Ideals to counteract an increasing tendency of another group to belittle American values (while hypocritically deriving great benefits by paying lip service to those values).

Motion picture director Sam Wood was the first Alliance president, followed by Clark Gable, Robert Taylor, and, in 1949, John Wayne. As a board member of the Screen Actors Guild during the 1940s, he had become aware of the so-called liberal influence. He recalls that, "once you get sensitized to it, you'd begin to be aware of cracks at our President, the flag, God, patriotism. A kind of sneering."

But it was not until *Back To Bataan* that he came up against the real thing. Maurice Zolotow in his book *Shooting Star* quotes Wayne's recollections:

"I didn't attend the first few meetings of the Alliance, because I was making *Back To Bataan*, which Edward Dmytryk was directing for RKO. I had been asked by our State Department to make this movie because it was about the Filipino underground. Our technical adviser was an American colonel, one of the first to get out of the Philippines. He was a religious man and a very sincere patriot. On days when I wasn't on the set, a few men—including Eddie Dmytryk—were ragging him about God, singing the *Internationale*, and making jokes about patriotism."

When confronted by Wayne, Dmytryk pretended it was all a joke. Later, of course, the director took the Fifth Amendment and went to jail only to emerge as a born-again patriot anxious to fink on his former comrades.

Later in his career Wayne talks about his political orientation. "I have found a certain type calls himself a liberal . . . now I always thought I was a liberal. I came up terribly surprised one time when I found out that I was a right-wing, conservative extremist, when I have listened to everybody's point of view that I ever met, and then decided how I should feel. But this so-called new liberal group, Jesus, they never listen to your point of view . . ."

13.
DUKE VS. THE JAPS AND CHATA

There is the rare motion picture star who is able to fit himself inside almost any characterization; Laurence Olivier and Jack Nicholson come to mind. One of the secrets of Duke's longevity is that he could be objective enough about himself to know the range into which he could fit comfortably. He didn't always know it going into a picture, especially in the old days, but—as he might say—he sure as hell knew it coming out, and seldom repeated the mistake.

The star also understood the director's vital role. He studied directors the way other actors studied their own press releases, and concluded that a director had to have an actor's total trust in order to extract the best possible performance from him.

"I'll tell you the difference between directors," Duke reminisces. "(Howard) Hawks has tremendous patience with people. He'll keep working on a fellow, even if he's not cutting the mustard. (John) Ford won't hire you unless he knows he can get it out of you. (William) Wellman figures you're a pro and doesn't bother you much as an actor, he'll simply cut the part down. It's that easy."

Wayne always put himself entirely in John Ford's hands and *They Were Expendable*, a superior 1945 war film co-starring Robert Montgomery and Donna Reed, was an obvious result. There is a story that when Wayne, a civilian because of his age and dependents despite several attempts to enlist, met with P.T. boat commander Lieutenant Robert Montgomery and Lieutenant Commander John Ford, both in their naval uniforms, to discuss the picture, he was so overcome with emotion that he had to leave the room to weep over his shame at not fighting for his country.

It is hard to imagine a sober John Wayne doing something like that, but whatever its genesis the picture stands up well to this day. Montgomery gives one of his real laid-back performances as a P.T. squadron commander in the early days of the American retreat in the Pacific, with Wayne as a hotheaded subordinate wanting to take on the then overwhelmingly dominant Japanese navy. Bataan falls and Wayne's boat is sunk by a Jap cruiser. He and Montgomery are ordered back to Washington to organize new squadrons that will be better able to take on the enemy. Wayne doesn't want to leave the scene of battle, but when Montgomery quietly asks, "Who are you working for? Yourself?" Wayne sensibly acquiesces and boards the last plane to leave the battle zone. That final touch has to be pure Ford, establishing the Wayne screen image of rugged individuality coupled with a sense of higher purpose.

Without Reservations, an otherwise undistinguished 1946 film is memorable for one line Duke speaks to Claudette Colbert. The story is about two marine officers, Wayne and Don DeFore, who meet novelist Colbert on a train heading West where her book is going to be filmed in Hollywood. The chemistry between Wayne and Colbert didn't produce the light wit that was intended, Wayne wasn't sure of Director Mervyn LeRoy and vice versa, but

*THEY WERE EXPENDABLE (1945) co-starring Robert Montgomery and
Donna Reed, was one of the better war films. Off screen,
Wayne had just divorced his first wife and was depressed
about not being able to join the armed forces.*

*WITHOUT RESERVATIONS (1946) co-starring Claudette Colbert with
Don DeFore and Anne Triola was meant to be a comedy.
Some of the lines were amusing only if you knew that Duke
had just married second wife Esperanza Baur.*

it does have a suggestion of women's lib in Colbert's sophisticated woman of the world who meets men on their own terms. Wayne will have none of that and tells her, "I want a woman who needs me, who's helpless and cute."

What makes the line nothing short of hilarious in hindsight is that he had just married Esperanza Baur. He had lured Chata to Hollywood with the promise that she would become a movie star, and, in fact, she was screen-tested and showed promise. Then he made mistake number one: He put her home on the shelf to be his woman and not get mixed up in show business. That led to mistake number two: Agreeing to let Esperanza's mother, Senora Ceballos, live with them to keep her daughter company.

Chata was not one of your model, apron-wearing, keep-the-dindin-warm, passive wives. The trouble started almost immediately because Wayne spent so much time either working on pictures, or in various offices and saloons talking about pictures.

Chata drank, and Chata swore, and Chata accused Wayne of sleeping with his pictures instead of with her. To placate her, Duke invited her mother up from Mexico. Chata's mother drank, and swore, and accused her son-in-law of all manner of infidelities.

To say that the seven-year marriage was stormy is like calling World War II a scuffle. Mama went back to Mexico in 1949, then Chata began disappearing from the Wayne home in Encino, a San Fernando Valley suburb of Los Angeles, for months at a time. Duke's old friend, publicist Jim Henaghen, was publicly quoted as saying that Chata's mother was "a crazy broad" who wanted to take the star for "a bundle." There seems little question but that Wayne loved Chata; he tried to reconcile their differences several

Who says pictures don't lie? This quiet, coffee-sipping domestic scene with the new Mrs. Wayne and her mother Senora Ceballos hardly reflected the true situation.

times (once at the muzzle end of a black automatic a half-drunk Chata held pointed at his chest) but divorce was inevitable.

Chivalrous to a fault, the star told his lawyer to "give her anything she wants" to avoid a messy public confrontation, but Chata would have none of it. She hired attorney Jerry Giesler, and had her day in court in November, 1953. Wayne denied any infidelity, specifically defending his relationship with Gail Russell, the dark-haired beauty who had been his co-star in *Angel and the Badman* and *Wake of the Red Witch*.

To Chata's charges that he had "clobbered" her, and generally physically abused her, Wayne, under oath and looking pale and dispirited, replied, "I had to keep up the public relations for us. It was humiliating to have her get drunk in nightclubs, fall down, cause disturbances at parties. It affected my work."

As to who clobbered whom, the star testified, "Many times I had to hold her arms and grab her foot when she was trying to strike or kick me." A reporter covering the trial noted that Wayne's face became flushed when he further testified that while he was in Honolulu on location for *Big Jim McLain* she had entertained hotel heir Nicky Hilton in their home. Chata, admitting that Nicky had occupied a guest room for a week, denied any wrongdoing.

Wayne agreed to pay her one hundred and fifty thousand dollars immediately, to settle her debts up to that time, and to pay her fifty thousand dollars a year for six years. Sometime in 1954, scarcely one year after the settlement, Esperanza Wayne, reportedly drinking heavily and living as a recluse, died in a hotel room in Mexico City.

*"He doesn't give any scenes away,
but he's fair."* — *Montgomery Clift*

14.

GAIL RUSSELL

John Wayne's discipline as an actor is never more apparent than during his Chata period. He drank his share, raised some hell, fought a losing battle on the home front, and made some extremely good motion pictures.

Although a critical failure—the New York Post's Archer Winsten called it "... an outrageous waste of time, celluloid, and productive ambition"—*Angel and the Badman* had its good points, and as usual Duke learned something from it. His first picture as a producer, it paired him with Gail Russell in the, for him, different role of a gunfighter who is persuaded to hang up his weapon, and in the final shootout is saved by a marshal who has come to arrest him.

Directed by writer James Edward Grant, the film was very slow-moving, featuring a lot of reaction shots: Close-ups of Wayne reacting to Miss Russell, or Harry Carey, Sr. who played the marshal, or Bruce Cabot who played the bad guy.

Wayne understood the reason for the picture's failure. Always

ANGEL AND THE BADMAN (1947) was Wayne's first as a producer.
Both co-star Gail Russell and writer James Edward Grant
would have strong impacts on Wayne's life.

the professional he saw that long successions of intimate scenes
expressing subtle nuances of character were not for him. Although Grant would stay on as the star's resident dialogue writer
for a number of years, Wayne demonstrated his objectivity about
his screen image by never again permitting the man who was one
year his senior to direct a picture of his.

The character we automatically accept today as John Wayne
made his first screen appearance in *Fort Apache* in 1948. The first
of three Wayne starrers—the others were *She Wore A Yellow
Ribbon* and *Rio Grande*—that John Ford made about the U.S.
Cavalry, the picture that firmly established the screen personality that persists to this day also saw the star outgunned artisti-

cally by co-star (with second billing) Henry Fonda. True, Fonda's character based on General George Custer was central to the film; even so it is the only time that Wayne, on his home turf inhabited by horses, rifles, Indians, and the great American West, is beaten to the drawl by another actor.

Red River was next and, as we've already discussed, solidified Duke's frim grasp on himself as an actor who was acquiring the self-discipline and awareness needed to keep him at the top of his profession. Aside from Bosley Crowther, critics who praised the picture, director Howard Hawks, and newcomer Montgomery Clift, largely ignored John Wayne. In a way their omissions were the highest compliments, although it hardly seemed that way to

An early scene from RED RIVER featuring Walter Brennan and Mickey Kuhn as a young Montgomery Clift. This 1948 acting milestone for Wayne stirred up a swirl of critical dust.

*A later RED RIVER scene with Joanne Dru showing how
Duke aged in the picture. As an actor he was more
than up to the difficult role.*

the star at the time. He was getting so good at his craft that everyone simply took for granted that he wasn't acting at all! He stands tall, solid, reassuring, and predictable, pulling the characters and plot along in his wake so that John McCarten of *The New Yorker* saw *Red River* as an "utterly satisfactory cowpunching drama," without once publicly asking himself "Why?"

Three Godfathers followed *Red River* in 1949. Directed by Ford, it is one of those pictures that makes you shake your head. It's about three likable outlaws, Wayne, Pedro Armendariz, and Harry Carey, Jr., who rob a bank and become unwitting godfathers to a newly-born infant; the film ends up with two of the robbers dead, and Duke off to the slammer. The picture is part

Pedro Armendariz and Harry Carey, Jr., with his arm in a sling, make up the other two of the THREE GODFATHERS in 1949. A rare instance of a John Ford directed John Wayne picture not making much sense.

According to testimony in Wayne's second divorce proceeding in 1954, Gail Russell didn't do much pushing away after the camera stopped. Here they star in WAKE OF THE RED WITCH in 1949.

*WAKE OF THE RED WITCH co-star Gig Young stands well over six feet,
but looks much smaller beside Wayne. One reason why many
leading men refused to appear with the big star.*

put-on, part comedy, part pure tragedy, and part Ford outdoor
realism.

The viewer never knows whether to laugh or cry. Wayne, a
complete stranger, is improbably made town marshal on his way
to rob the bank. After the successful holdup a pursuing posse
wounds Harry Carey, Jr., but all three get away. They chance on a
covered wagon in which Mildred Natwick (in a step-up from her
Long Voyage Home whore), a frontier woman abandoned by her
husband, is giving birth. She extracts a promise from Wayne to
look after the child and promptly expires.

Now we have laugh lines as the three rough gunmen take care
of the kid. Then in rapid succession Harry Carey, Jr. dies from his
wound, and Pedro Armendariz hurts himself so badly that Wayne
has to abandon him after giving him a gun with which to do away

with himself when the going gets tough. No more laughs.

Wayne then turns up in town, is arrested after making sure the baby is cared for, given a trial and sentenced. But no one is really sore at anyone and there is a big drunken party to see Wayne off at the train taking him to prison. It's a tribute to Duke that he carries off the confusing portrayal with some believability. Not much; but some. *Time* magazine's review summed up the general consensus when it called the picture an "unintentional parody of the old-fashioned western."

Like so many of his pictures, John Wayne's next for Republic, *Wake of the Red Witch*, had off-screen implications even more dramatic than the film story. When Chata found out that his co-star was once again to be Gail Russell, one can imagine that the stormy seas on the home front matched or exceeded those threatening the ship Red Witch on the screen. Looking at Miss Russell's delicate vulnerable beauty, it is easy to believe that in the story she becomes fatally ill and welcomes death as a release from a tormented marriage to Luther Adler's character. It is not as easy to accept that, in real life, she was even then caught in the throes of personal uncertainties and demons that would lead to her death from alcoholism in 1961 at the age of thirty-six.

Wake of the Red Witch is a sea story with some of the elements of *Reap the Wild Wind*. There is sunken treasure; Wayne fights an octopus (and wins, this time); after bargaining his services for first mate Gig Young's freedom, he loses his own life; at fade out, he is united with Gail after death, sailing off on the Red Witch into the sunset. It's all very melodramatic and, as directed by Edward Ludwig, difficult to believe; the Batjak Trading Company in the film was taken by Wayne as the name for his own Batjac Productions, probably the film's most memorable contribution to even a limited posterity.

 ACADEMY AWARD NOMINATION

John the Baptist had Salome and John the Wayne had Vera Hruba.

The second John's travails began when Herbert J. Yates, the sixty-one-year-old head of Republic, fell in love with blond ice skater Vera Hruba Ralston. Remember how the Studios used to get away with those shots of Sonja Henie in micro-minis and tights? Well Vera Hruba had a great bod that showed to extreme advantage in *Ice Capades*, a film she starred in for Republic.

Mr. Yates was torn between heart and head. He knew that his little love-bunch couldn't act, and that casting her with his top star John Wayne would protect her on the screen. What he wasn't at all that certain about was how she would be protected from Duke off-screen. But he wanted her name up in lights; the best way to accomplish that without losing his shirt was to team her with

Wayne. First in *Dakota*, then in *The Fighting Kentuckian*, Vera Hruba demonstrated that as an actress she was a great skater.

Both pictures made money (as, allegedly, seven others she made without Duke did not) but Yates, who would make an honest woman of Vera Hruba in 1953, was rumored to be in constant anguish at her proximity to his top male star. About that time Duke, switching his affections from Josie to Chata, had his hands full, but Yates still wasn't sure; one report from the set had Wayne trying to help straighten out the well-stacked blonde's European accent; it apparently nearly gave the studio head, forty years her senior, a heart attack. Duke, of course, knew what was going on, he enjoyed himself immensely in Yates's company,

*There is more to this picture with Vera Hruba Ralston
in THE FIGHTING KENTUCKIAN (1949) than meets the eye.*

Smiles for the camera at Republic in 1949. Studio boss Herbert J. Yates
on left was worried about the future Mrs. Yates (Vera Hruba)
being around Duke. On right is Republic board member Buster Mills.

compensating for being saddled professionally with an untrained filly by letting the older man sweat out his uncertainties.

Five John Wayne films were released in 1949, a prodigious output of such uneven quality that we must marvel at the public's penchant for recalling only the good times in the star's career. Those good times were epitomized by the fourth film of that year, *She Wore A Yellow Ribbon*. The second of John Ford's U.S. Cavalry trilogy, it takes up where *Fort Apache* left off, with Custer and his men massacred at the Little Big Horn; the entire western frontier seethed with Indian unrest that threatened to escalate into an extended war.

Wayne's Captain Nathan Brittles, charged with the job of turning the Indian tide, is a direct fictional descendant of *Red River*'s Thomas Dunson. A forty-year Army man about to be retired, Brittles is at once firm, knowing, fair, and fearless, all without being the stereotypical "Army man" that would have made his role dull and uninteresting. The film is also marked by his unusual paternal relationship with a beautiful young woman. He looks on with knowing amusement as Joanne Dru is courted by both John Agar and Harry Carey, Jr.; but director Ford doesn't let us forget whom we're watching. When Joanne Dru pins a yellow ribbon on her dress as a sign that she has chosen a sweetheart, Wayne asks her to name the lucky man. He roars with laughter when she replies coquettishly, "Why, for you, of course, Captain Brittles," but there is a moment when we see a flash of the male sexual appeal that shows through the characterization.

This picture should have put to rest any doubts about Wayne's

From left John Howard, Hugo Haas, and Philip Dorn confront Wayne and Jack Pennick on a Republic sound stage. Painted backdrops that are realistic in a motion picture often show up badly in still photographs.

*John Agar and Joanne Dru co-star in SHE WORE A YELLOW RIBBON
in 1949. Wayne's finest acting job since RED RIVER, as
Captain Brittles he gradually grows away from romantic leads.*

acting ability. White at the temples, sporting a graying, shaggy moustache, the star is not merely portraying Brittles, he *is* Brittles, every bit as believable as was Henry Fonda as Custer's character in *Fort Apache*. The viewer can't help but speculate what would have happened had Captain Brittles confronted Fonda's General Custer in that picture. Or, indeed, why did he not? The answer, perhaps, is that Wayne's *Fort Apache* character, Captain Kirby York, made his appearance before *Red River* and the year-and-a-half separating the York and Brittles roles represented an extraordinary maturing of the actor's talents. Wayne's drinking buddy Victor McLaglen turns in an especially effective performance as Brittles's worshipful, though needling, sergeant.

That John Wayne should have won his first Academy Award nomination for his next picture *Sands of Iwo Jima* (with John Agar and Forrest Tucker) and not for *She Wore a Yellow Ribbon* speaks ill of the nominators' perceptions. His peers, like his public, took his seeming naturalness on the screen for granted. "He could do that western routine in his sleep," a newspaper reviewer commented. But, of course, that was not so. Back with *The Three Mesquiteers*, *mebbe*, but not from *Red River* on.

Wayne plays an actor's dream part in his last 1949 picture, *Sands of Iwo Jima*, a tough, battle-hardened Marine Corps sergeant with a heart, if not of gold, at least malleable enough to leave a

One of Hollywood's longest lasting professional and personal relationships is reflected in this scene with Victor McLaglen in SHE WORE A YELLOW RIBBON.

Captain Nathan Brittles, United States Cavalry, at your service.

With Forrest Tucker in a supporting role, SANDS OF IWO JIMA brought
Wayne his first Academy Award nomination.

*The war picture was tremendously popular. When he lost out
to Broderick Crawford for the Oscar, Wayne fans flocked
to the theaters in even greater numbers.*

whore unpenetrated when he learns that she is supporting a little
baby lying in a crib in the next room. Not only that, he gives her
money and stays to help prepare the kid's formula! It's one of those
times that, with a big assist from Allan Dwan's carefully controlled
direction, the big man makes a believer out of us in a situation that
could easily degenerate into unwitting comedy.

That scene is Academy Award material and Wayne's portrayal of Sergeant John M. Stryker, a by-the-book Marine, but a
troubled and at times depressed man (a state he relieves by
indulging in a tried-and-true drinking bout), probably merited
the nomination. He is killed at picture's end, a shockingly harsh,
abrupt death from a single sniper's bullet, just when he appears
to be letting down the cold, professional facade that separated
him from his men.

The picture was exceptionally popular with a public still riding the crest of a wave of patriotic fervor following the Second World War. When Broderick Crawford won the Oscar for *All The King's Men*, crowds lined up to see Wayne's movie took the vote as being downright un-American. The *New York Times* critic noted that "Wayne is especially honest and convincing . . . His performance holds the picture together."

An illustration of Wayne's continuing debt to Yakima Canutt comes to light in Peter Bogdanovich's book *Allan Dwan, The Past Pioneer* when the writer asked the director how Wayne took direction in the fight scenes that were so much a part of his screen personality.

"He's particularly good at faking punches," Dwan replied. "I let him and Forrest Tucker slug it out. They'd talk over their fight scenes and work them out. And I know one time these two young actors weren't doing exactly what I wanted . . . And all of a sudden, over my shoulder, Wayne said, 'God damn it! Will you bastards do what he tells you?' And they did it then. I said, 'Thanks.' "

James Grant was brought in by Wayne to rewrite some of his dialogue and Dwan wasn't too happy about it. "He (Wayne) seemed to think that Grant was the only man who could put the words the way he ought to say them," the director observed.

*"He brings to each new movie . . .
a sense of the past."
— Peter Bogdanovich*

16.
A THIRD MARRIAGE

Rio Grande, Wayne's first 1950 release, and the last of Ford's three U.S. Cavalry pictures, pairs him for the first time with Maureen O'Hara and is perhaps the least distinguished of the three. An interesting sidelight is the appearance in a minor role of Ken Curtis who would later go on to T.V. stardom as Festus Hagen, Jim Arness's memorable deputy on *Gunsmoke*. J. Carrol Naish is cast, or miscast, as General Philip Sheridan, Wayne's commanding officer who orders his subordinate to illegally chase Indians across the Mexican border.

Despite taking an arrow in the chest, pulled out by his son Jeff played by Claude Jarman, Jr., Wayne lives happily ever after. The minor irritations of the Naish casting, the improbable arrow-pulling scene, and one or two other plot coincidences tend to reduce the impact of Ford's action direction. Wayne is noble and brave and his own man—defying an international treaty because of his personal loyalty to Sheridan—but it all seems somehow stuck together without the strong central themes of *Fort Apache* and *She Wore A Yellow Ribbon*.

Howard Hughes, then RKO chief executive, displayed consummate bad timing and equally bad taste by trying for another *Sands of Iwo Jima* with a picture titled *Flying Leathernecks*. Wayne, feeling protected by the hiring of writer James Edward Grant, lets himself be cast in the unsympathetic role of a marine fighter squadron commander in the Pacific in 1942. Unlike his more popular second in command, played by Robert Ryan (an unusual casting for the frequently "bad guy" actor), Wayne has the toughness to send his men into battle against what he knows to be suicidal odds.

Confronting Indians seems a way of life for the star and
RIO GRANDE (1950) is no exception. Some of these scenes
would come back to haunt him in later years.

With co-star Robert Ryan and Adam Williams in
FLYING LEATHERNECKS (1951). Wayne, to his surprise, found
that the public reacted negatively to his role.

Three or four years previously Wayne would have been applauded and Ryan, who quotes the classics, labeled some kind of a liberal misfit, but the movie audience was rapidly becoming escapist and someone who sent men to their deaths—even if he was John Wayne—did not set well.

In a recent interview, now film director Bogdanovich talks about Wayne's impact on a picture. "He brings to each new movie—good or bad—a resonance and a sense of the past—his own and ours—that fills it with reverberations above and beyond its own perhaps limited qualities. That is the true measure of what makes a great movie star . . ."

An indication of how many things were wrong with *Flying*

Leathernecks is the fact that it was one of the rare times that the post *Red River* Wayne not only didn't save the picture, but ended up with the audience feeling uneasy about his characterization.

You don't have to be Irish to enjoy *The Quiet Man*, but it helps. John Ford took every brogue in Hollywood, Maureen O'Hara, Barry Fitzgerald, Victor McLaglen, Ward Bond, Arthur Shields, Sean McClory, Jack McGowran, and—the saints preserve us—Ken Curtis (Festus again) as an Irish ballad singer, to support Wayne in what one critic described as "the longest build-up to a fistfight and a piece of ass in film history."

Well, now, it was a bit more than that, surely; yet it did feature lots of scenery. Despite Ford's great capacity for movement, it remains essentially a love story that does climax in a fight scene between Wayne and McLaglen, followed by O'Hara giving Duke the hottest come-hither look this side of Lauren Bacall in *To Have and Have Not*.

John Wayne's first picture as a producer-star for Warner Bros. in 1952 probably did more to encourage the exaggerated image of his reactionary politics than anything he said for publication. *Big Jim McLain* as played by Wayne, is an investigator for the House Un-American Activities Committee who, with fellow investigator and war hero Mal Baxter (played by James Arness), sets out to uncover a Communist spy ring in Hawaii. It is doubtful that even Ronald Reagan would have let himself get trapped into this picture.

Wayne has been quoted here as saying he listens to all sides of an argument; well, in *Big Jim McLain* his character does not. McLain says: "There are a lot of wonderful things written into our constitution but they're meant for honest, decent citizens and I resent the fact that it can be used and abused by the very people that want to destroy it." A lot of thinking people resent it, too, but know that it's a necessary risk if our society is to survive.

Perhaps the fact that he was having so much trouble with Chata (she was keeping house with Nicky Hilton at the time) distracted the star, and had him give writer James Grant too much leeway. In any case the script was so blatant in missing the subtleties of the Communist ideological influence that it alienated people who considered themselves good Americans, but who didn't want crude propaganda shoved down their throats.

*A surprise birthday party for 13-year-old son Patrick on
the set of BIG JIM MCLAIN in 1952 as his
17-year-old brother Michael looks on.*

Then, once again as his own producer under the Wayne-Fellows imprint, Duke made another clinker. *Island in the Sky* is about a transport-plane pilot who makes an emergency landing on a frozen lake and keeps up his crew's spirits until help arrives. That's it. A static, talky version of Ernest K. Gann's novel, the picture once again had James Arness in a minor role. About this time Wayne took the unusual step of signing the future Matt Dillon to a personal contract, seeing in the young actor the possibility of molding someone in the now middle-aged star's own image.

That gut instinct, honed by experience and aided by his own intelligence, had Wayne put himself back in the saddle after his less-than-mediocre beginnings as a producer. James Edward Grant who, like his mentor, only seemed truly at ease with a big picture western and dialogue, had written *Hondo* to be produced by Wayne-Fellows and directed by John Farrow. Several leads were being considered, among them Glenn Ford, but Wayne read the script, and took the part for his own.

The strength of the resulting film is manifest by the fact that it was filmed as a 3-D exploitation picture (remember the little green and blue glasses we had to look through at the screen?), but has become a flat-screen minor classic.

The picture abounds with memorable John Wayne scenes: Wayne as ex-gunfighter now cavalry scout Hondo Lane, his horse shot from under him by Indians, striding with his saddle and Winchester—shades of the Ringo Kid in *Stagecoach*—toward apprehensive ranch house owner Geraldine Page and her son; Wayne spread-eagled on the ground being tortured by Indians who set burning coals on his hands; Wayne in a knife fight with an Indian whom he beats but spares; Wayne's little dog ruthlessly gutted by an Indian lance, and Hondo finally sticking the Indian in like manner.

Wayne, discussing his problems with the modern Indian movement referred to his Hondo Indian as a good guy; in all fairness it should be pointed out that there was one good and one bad Indian, the latter getting his just deserts not because of his race but because of his behavior.

Hondo had all of Duke's basic story ingredients, "a dog, a kid, a woman's love," and he made the best of them with a great assist from Broadway actress Geraldine Page in her first movie role. Interestingly, Katharine Hepburn was considered for the part; it would be twenty-two years before Hepburn and Wayne were teamed in *Rooster Cogburn*.

James Arness was cast in a minor role as he was again when Wayne hit the deck in *The Sea Chase* co-starring Lana Turner with young actor Tab Hunter in a supporting role. Wayne is a good German (in those days the distinctions were clear) in this Second World War story of a German freighter being pursued by a British warship. Lana Turner is a beautiful German spy (what else?) and Lyle Bettger a ruthless Nazi who is taken care of by Wayne before The End.

This is about the extent of the action in ISLAND IN THE SKY (1953). Here, with Sean McClory, Wayne may be privately deploring the picture's lack of plot.

Broadway actress Geraldine Page in her first screen role.
Originally filmed in 3-D, HONDO remains as one of
Wayne's finest characterizations.

Collectors of memorable lines might like to add to a list that
stretches back to when pre-tough guy Humphrey Bogart, playing
in *Meet The Wife*, a light comedy on Broadway, bounds onstage in
white flannels, carrying a tennis racket, and poses the now im-
mortal question, "Tennis anyone?" In *The Sea Chase* Duke, gazing
earnestly into Lana Turner's eyes, drawls, "Did anyone ever tell
you you're beautiful when you're angry?" It was that kind of a
picture.

As we have seen, Duke's professional life bore little relationship to his private one. He could be embroiled with Chata and
make fine pictures; conversely he could make a disappointing
film like *The Sea Chase* while his personal life was never better. In
1951 while on a trip to Peru he had met a striking Pan-American

Grace Airways stewardess named Pilar Palette Weldy. Although she was married at the time, she no longer lived with her husband, and was getting a few small parts in locally produced motion pictures.

In what was almost a replay of his Chata romance, he returned home only to meet Pilar again in Hollywood at a cocktail party. Leaving Chata in possession he had moved out of his Encino house. Pilar seemed everything that Chata was not; it wasn't long before they were dating regularly. *Motion Picture*, a fan magazine, would dutifully report that, "John Wayne woke up in the morning and he realized he wasn't in love with Esperanza any

The real action was off screen during THE SEA CHASE filming in 1954. The recently divorced star, here with Lyle Bettger and Lana Turner, wed his third wife Pilar Palette on location in Honolulu right after the shooting was completed.

more, and he knew he had fallen in love with Pilar.'' The account didn't say which morning, but however it happened Wayne waited for his divorce, asked for Pilar's hand (she, too, had divorced Panagra publicity man Dick Weldy) and was accepted.

Filming on *The Sea Chase* on location in Hawaii was completed at the end of October, 1954; Duke and Pilar were married on November 1 in Honolulu. They returned to Los Angeles where Pilar moved into the Encino house long vacated by Chata and her mother. One of Wayne's beefs had been that Chata would only hire Spanish-speaking servants and he never knew what was going on; Pilar immediately hired three Peruvian, Spanish-speaking servants. Pilar was a Roman Catholic, and a man of the cloth was soon in attendance blessing each room in the house. So Duke was once again surrounded by foreigners and having his bed sprinkled with holy water. But he was very much in love and these first faint remembrances of things past failed to diminish his happiness.

17.
BACALL, HAYWARD AND O'HARA

Only John Wayne could substitute a composite of the most beautiful girls he had known for God, and get away with it. That's just what he did in *Blood Alley* in which he co-starred with Lauren Bacall in 1955. The Communist Chinese are the heavies as Wayne, a soldier-of-fortune type merchant-ship skipper is persuaded by a Chinese village doctor's daughter, Lauren Bacall, to help all 180 villagers escape from the Reds down "Blood Alley," the three-hundred-mile Formosa Straits.

For some reason known only to the screenwriter, Wayne has a habit of raising his eyes heavenward and addressing "Babe," a presence comprising the best features of his girls in every port. Come to think of it, Duke's outspoken asides to Babe may be a plot

The Chinese Communists are the bad guys in BLOOD ALLEY released in 1955. A seemingly ideal casting of Lauren Bacall as his co-star didn't quite come off on the screen.

convenience, as when he allows as how "The bleeding heart of China—you can pin one on my sleeve, Babe," tells us of his commitment against the commies, and the sympathy that motivates him taking all those chances.

Wayne's newly formed production company Batjac first offered this role to Humphrey Bogart, but he wanted too much money. Bacall does her best as she belatedly takes Babe's place in Wayne's affections but the whole thing ends up as a slightly more credible version of *The Sea Chase*. An intriguing bit of casting has a Chinese girl Wei Ling played by newcomer Anita Ekberg, a role that required the blond future star to play down her more obvious talents.

When John Wayne observed that he had made more bad pictures than anyone who survived in Hollywood he must surely have been thinking about *The Conqueror* in which he plays Genghis Khan. Even the simple casting announcement sounds like a laugh line. As directed by crooner turned movie private eye turned director, Dick Powell, this story of the Mongol Genghis Khan and his hots for beautiful Bortoi (Susan Hayward), daughter of a Tartar chief, defies rational review. It's as though everyone got together and devised a series of situations and dialogue that would make Wayne look ludicrous.

An enormous cast and a five million dollar budget went right down the tube—the late movie television tube—as theater audiences stayed away in hordes. For perhaps the only time in his professional career Wayne looked like an idiot in his spiked helmet and funny little wisps of moustache. To make matters worse, braves from the Chivwit Indian tribe played Mongolian warriors and many of Hollywood's regular western actors had supporting roles. You haven't experienced high camp until you've seen Lee Van Cleef and William Conrad as Tartar and/or Mongol, choose one. Or until you've heard Wayne tell a defiant Hayward, "You're beautiful in your wrath."

That's Susan Hayward co-starred in THE CONQUEROR, a 1956 absurdity.

*A pause during the filming of THE WINGS OF EAGLES (1957)
as Navy flyer Wayne, fist cocked, waits until Army flyer
Kenneth Tobey gets some cake out of his eye before director
John Ford calls for "Action," resuming the fight.*

Then, wonder of wonders, in that same 1956 John Wayne
starred in *The Searchers*, in retrospect one of his best and most
underrated pictures. Back in the western saddle again, Wayne
gives an outstanding performance as a man bent on avenging the
Indian slaughter of a family and on recovering two young nieces
carried off by the raiders. The search takes five years, and when
Wayne finally finds the only living survivor, Natalie Wood, the
fact that she has become a Comanche squaw makes her so un-
clean and morally degraded in his eyes that his instinctive solution is to kill her. It is his most anti-Indian film.

Wayne's evolution from Confederate officer to drifter, to bank

*Nothing like a dip in the pool to show it's all in fun. Peering over
Wayne's right shoulder is Ken Curtis, later to win television
acclaim as Festus Hagen, Matt Dillon's deputy on GUNSMOKE.*

robber, to sentimentalist, to Indian hater and, finally, to magnanimous dispenser of justice is simply a tremendous job of acting. Critics downplayed the picture when it was first released, but more recently a poll of 100 international film reviewers had seventy-eight percent of them putting the film in their list of all-time great pictures.

About this time James Arness stopped appearing in Wayne pictures, for a very good reason: A half-hour black and white television show titled *Gunsmoke* made its debut on the CBS network in 1955 starring Arness. Eventually expanded to an hour in color, the series ran for twenty years, making Arness the John Wayne of television westerns. Later in the series another Wayne screen regular, Ken Curtis, joined *Gunsmoke* as Matt Dillon's deputy Festus Hagen, in an unforgettable portrayal that, to date, has been the capstone of an astonishingly versatile acting career that began as one of the singing Sons of the Pioneers in Duke's old Republic days.

Wayne, who had Arness under personal contract, talks about the younger man's transition from big to small screen. "The network wanted me to do a series and I said no but I had this fellow Jim Arness who would do a great job. I told them just to surround him with good people and they'd make him a star. So I made the deal and told Arness, 'I got it all set for you.'

"Well, he pulls this long face and tells me, 'Television! You're ruining my career!' So I said to him, 'Your career? You sonofabitch, you can't get a job! Everybody says you're too big to work with. You know damn well I'm the only one'll work with you." So, reluctantly, James Arness went on to become a big star and a millionaire.

With Arness's television career launched, Wayne fictionally returned to the sea in *The Wings of Eagles*, based on the life of ex-naval flying hero Frank "Spig" Wead who, after being crippled by a fall downstairs in his home, became a writer. With some help from his navy buddy Lieutenant Commander John Ford (introduced to one another in the film by the ubiquitous Ken Curtis), Wead became a screenwriter and did the screenplay for *They Were Expendable*.

Some people say there are three biographies in *The Wings of Eagles*—Wead's, Ford's, and Wayne's. The John Ford character in

Wead's life is played on the screen by Ward Bond in, for him, an unusually demanding character role. Bond brings it off beautifully and there can be little doubt but that Ford, who directed the picture, was more than a little flattered at the way screenwriters Frank Fenton and William Wister Haines handled the director's role in the story.

In the film Wead is shown as a career navy man—"Star-Spangled Wead," screen wife Maureen O'Hara remarks bitterly—who places home and family a distant second to duty to his country. Crippled though he is, he resumes active duty during the Second World War and goes to sea on a carrier until his injuries prove too exhausting for him to continue. Some Wayne watchers draw a parallel between Wead and the screen star,

Maureen O'Hara shows a daring bit of leg as the wife of
THE WINGS OF EAGLES real life Navy hero Commander Frank
"Spig" Wead played by the man behind the wheel.

suggesting that both men put career above family obligations. That may be stretching it a bit, but Wayne plays Wead as a naval counterpart of himself, hard-drinking, patriotic, and outspoken, and the fictional portrayal is an obvious reflection of Wayne's admiration for the man who pioneered carrier-based aviation.

18.

A COUPLE OF TURKEYS

Jet Pilot was the most expensive home movie ever made.

One of two Wayne films personally owned by Howard Hughes—the other was *The Conqueror*—it actually was filmed in 1950. The picture, released—the derogatory cliché "escaped" applies—in 1957, had nothing going for it but Hughes's misplaced enthusiasm, and some excellent aerial photography that was eventually cut drastically to reduce the running time.

Like *The Outlaw*, the film that starred Jane Russell, *Jet Pilot* was an expensive conceit for Hughes who produced it at RKO. The millionaire recluse saw himself in Wayne's title role of a test pilot who meets a defecting lady Russian test pilot (Janet Leigh) and the two perform a symbolic mating ritual in a dazzling display of aerobatics. It turns out that Leigh wasn't defecting at all, but was assigned to bring Duke back to Russia. She falls for

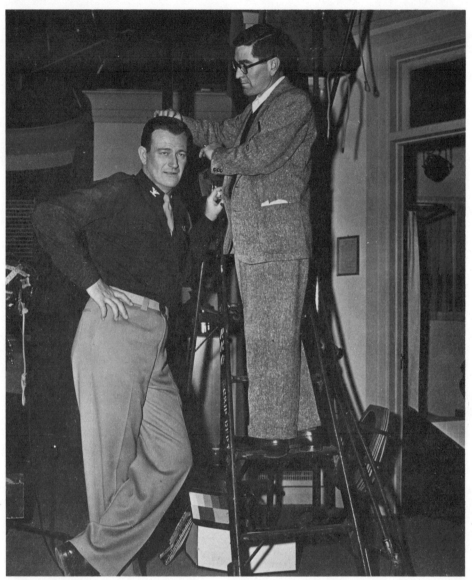

*The kind of publicity the studio had to stoop (or climb) to
for JET PILOT co-starring Janet Leigh, filmed in 1949 and finally
released in 1957. The climber is makeup man Web Overlander.*

A routine publicity shot for a routine motion picture.
JET PILOT, personally produced by Howard Hughes, is described
as the most expensive home movie ever made.

him, they stay in the U.S.A. and . . . well, it all works out. Hughes was said to have privately viewed the uncut version again and again, marveling at the photography and fantasizing as the screen hero.

Wayne's belief that an actor has to have complete faith in his director was put to the test in *The Barbarian and the Geisha*, and was found, to his and his audience's dismay, to be valid. He was cast as Townsend Harris, an American diplomat sent to Japan in 1856 to implement a trade treaty imposed on the isolationist Japanese by the threat of military intervention. Director John Huston professed to think that Wayne was right for the part; he told an interviewer, "I want to send Duke's gigantic form into the exotic world that was the Japanese empire in the 1800s . . . Who better to symbolize the big, awkward United States of one hundred years ago?"

From the beginning, Duke had doubts about the role. With Eiko Ando as the geisha and Sam Jaffe, the picture's only other occidental, as his interpreter, the big star was ill at ease with the costuming, the story's leisurely pace, and his inability to communicate with Huston. Duke had worked with many directors and had taken his lumps when a picture went bad, but he sensed in Huston an almost mocking tendency to destroy his image.

"I found it impossible," he said later, "to make any contact at all. When I look at his career, Bogey and his dad (Walter Huston) helped him get started; outside of *Moulin Rouge* and *The Asphalt Jungle*, I don't think he's made anything worthwhile when they weren't there to help him. Huston? You can have him."

For whatever reason, Wayne's instincts about the picture were right. *Time* magazine's summation, "Ouch—there goes three million bucks!" describes the picture's fate.

1959 was not proving to be one of Wayne's better years; straying too far from the western saddle, he was eroding both his popularity and his nerves. Asked by a fan magazine interviewer, "What has Van Johnson got that, in your opinion, you, unfortunately don't possess?" Duke replied, "Climb off my aching back," ending the interview, and encapsulating his professional frustrations.

Then he made *Rio Bravo*, his second picture with *Red River* director Howard Hawks. Whether it was the director, the locale, the cast, the character, the story, or a combination of all five, *Rio*

Here with Eiko Ando and Sam Jaffe in THE BARBARIAN AND THE GEISHA in 1958. One of the few times Wayne publicly expressed dissatisfaction with a director—in this case, John Huston.

Bravo was the kind of picture that the legion of John Wayne fans could sit back and simply enjoy. Wayne is a sheriff with a prisoner he has to keep in captivity and alive until proper justice can be dispensed. His Sheriff John T. Chance is courageous, realistic, and unbending—in short, pure John Wayne.

Surrounded by regulars like Walter Brennan, Ward Bond, Claude Akins, and Harry Carey, Jr., co-starred with Angie Dickinson and Dean Martin, Duke lets us relax and have a good time. Martin is surprisingly effective as Dude, a deputy gone to drink and resurrected by Wayne; then teen-idol Ricky Nelson acquits himself well as a Billy-the-Kid type gunslinger.

When he's on sure ground, Wayne can do almost anything and get away with it, as in one scene when he viciously smashes a gun butt in the face of a bad guy (a far cry from the old clean fighting hero days). Dean Martin, alarmed, cautions "Hey, take it easy." Wayne's reply "Aw, I'm not gonna hurt him," comes across as humor due solely to his presence and delivery. Western violence was escalating, and Wayne could sense just how much the audience would tolerate.

"Another beleaguered blockhouse western." — *Bosley Crowther,* THE NEW YORK TIMES

19.

THE ALAMO

1960 was the year of *The Alamo*. John Wayne was quoted as saying: "This picture is America. I hope that seeing the Battle of the Alamo will remind Americans that liberty and freedom don't come cheap."

Neither, he might have added, does making a film about those values.

Wayne had *The Alamo* on his mind for a long time before he finally produced and directed the picture. He was scouting possible locations for the film when he first met Pilar in Peru in 1951. Originally he had planned to play a small cameo role so that he could devote his full time to directing. When United Artists agreed to finance a major portion of the twelve million dollar budget, it was on condition that Wayne take a starring part.

He chose to play Davy Crockett, with Richard Widmark (Jim Bowie), Laurence Harvey (Colonel William Travis), and Richard Boone (General Sam Houston) as the other leads. Quite possibly he underestimated the magnitude of the task he had set for himself both artistically and financially. He ended up mortgaging his own Batjac company to come up with more than a million dollars to complete the picture, but more disastrously he spread himself too thin as actor, producer, and director.

Preparing for an epic of that size often occupies both a producer and a director full time in pre-production planning for as much as six months prior to the first scene being filmed. Producer-director Wayne did his pre-production work while filming *Rio Bravo* and *The Horse Soldiers*, both in themselves physically demanding pictures. Decisions on script (James Edward Grant was not only writer but associate producer), wardrobe, financing, the small town being built on location down in Brackettville, Texas, casting, as well as blocking scenes from a director's point-of-view—all these functions were handled at the end of a day's shooting (with his immediate lines and bits of business to be learned) from Hollywood and on location in Louisiana.

The pre-production costs were enormous, partly due to Wayne not being on the scene. Great herds of cattle and horses were assembled, an airfield built to supply the small army of extras, and the set itself outgrew the town. A *New York Times* man was impressed. He wrote that, ". . . few Hollywood films, even the great biblical spectacles, have had such extensive preparation for production."

But those preparations, while impressive visually, were deceptive. When the first frame of film was exposed in September 1959, John Wayne was an eager, happy, very tired fifty-two-year-old man. By all accounts he was a good director; he knew the script intimately, was sure of what he wanted, and got fine performances from Widmark and Harvey. He was everywhere, doing everything from checking the extras' costumes, to positioning lights, to rearranging props. And he smoked a lot more than usual, coughing up phlegm, and punishing his body mercilessly. He was up at the first light of dawn to begin shooting; at day's end promotion, publicity, and script conferences followed the showing of the daily rushes. Working late into the night, the screen image blended with the real man in a truly herculean three-month performance.

And for what? Reportedly not one cent of profit. Wayne claims that the stories of financial disaster were greatly exaggerated. He says that the picture made more than fifteen million dollars the first time around, a tidy sum for an ordinary picture but not enough for *The Alamo*. "I didn't make a cent on it," the star acknowledges, "because I made a bad goddamn deal."

Perhaps. However, others saw serious flaws in the picture itself. Writer Allen Eyles noted that "James Edward Grant's script is just not imaginative enough. It's cluttered and woolly . . . Certainly Grant's words are inadequate where the film's key speeches are concerned."

The action sequences were outstanding, but there were weaknesses in the interrelationships of the characters. You couldn't

Jim Bowie (Richard Widmark), Colonel William Travis (Laurence Harvey) stand with Davy Crockett who also produced and directed THE ALAMO in 1960. Depending on whom you asked, the picture either made or lost money.

Here checking Laurence Harvey's makeup, the star-director-producer was involved in every phase of the ambitious, expensive production, a reason given by some for the uneven result.

really hate the Mexicans storming the Alamo because, in truth, John Wayne didn't hate them, looking on them as brave soldiers fighting for the wrong cause. Motivation seemed lacking.

And if the picture itself was perhaps wanting in some areas, the publicity campaign added substantially to its burden. The Democratic and Republican parties were about to convene in preparation for the 1960 elections and someone—publicist Russell Birdwell was the most visible target—had the brilliant idea of comparing the deviousness of politicians with the patriotic purity of the men who gave their lives against General Santa Anna. So the advertising slogan *There were no ghostwriters at the Alamo. Only men.* was born. Tying in a commercial venture with the suggestion of ignoble motives on the part of the nation's political leaders hit the public the wrong way.

Although even critic Bosley Crowther, who had empathetically followed Wayne's career for so long, found the picture "another beleaguered blockhouse western," the public went to see it, but not in sufficient numbers to make it a substantial financial success. The picture was nominated in eleven categories for the Academy Awards (not including best director or actor) and won only one: Best sound. Imagine that—best sound. It was a slap in the face that some people felt was at least partly engineered by those who still resented Wayne's outspokenness against leftist influence in the industry. No one will ever really know.

THE COMANCHEROS (1961) provided Stuart Whitman, seen
crouching beside Pat Wayne, with one of his best roles, and
showed Duke's comedic sense.

"He's ready to bust ass. And he expects everybody else to bust ass." — Strother Martin

20.
TALL IN THE SADDLE

Right after the furor caused by *The Alamo* had died down, a disillusioned, embittered John Wayne was interviewed by John P. Nugent for *Newsweek* magazine. Knowing what we do now about his hard work, financial commitments, and the bad judgment shown in merchandising the picture, it is easier to understand one of the most un-John Wayne quotes ever attributed to him.

"If you're phony to your audience," the star is reported as saying, "you'll hurt your career. I don't owe a gawdam thing to my fans, but I do owe something to my pocketbook." Is that *our* John Wayne speaking? The man we root for, admire, the man who does the selfless thing, and earns our respect? He doesn't owe us "a gawdam thing?" We can almost hear the legions of fans who sat through the real dogs, paying their money secure in the knowledge that Duke would entertain them the next time, or the next after that, pleading, "Say it isn't so, Duke."

But it was so. Asked if too much television had hurt *The Alamo* (*Gunsmoke* was now a national obsession), he opined: "On TV the cowboy is introverted and oversensitive. The (real) cowboy loved, hated, had fun, was lusty. He didn't have mental problems."

It was easy to suggest that those real cowboys, as played by Wayne, didn't have the capacity to have mental problems, but all was soon forgiven when Duke came up with two pictures in 1961 that freed him from behind the camera and, as an actor, let him do what he knew best. The first was *The Comancheros*, a story about a Texas Ranger who breaks up an outlaw band. The plot was simple but the characterizations by writers Clair Huffaker and, give him his due, James Edward Grant were excellent.

Wayne, of course, is the Ranger who has Stuart Whitman first as his prisoner then, through a plot twist, his ally in a final glorious shootout raid on the renegades' armed camp. Whitman's Paul Regret, gambler, adventurer, man of the world, is one of his best parts, due in no small measure to his being able to play off against Wayne's strong presence. Regret, wanted for murder, tries to bribe and outsmart Wayne only to be told, "I wouldn't try any city-slicker stuff on this poor old country boy."

Lee Marvin, as hard-drinking, gambling Tully Crow makes his first big impression as a screen heavy, shading his characterization so that, when he is finally gunned down by Wayne, we react with mixed feelings. Ina Balin plays Pilar, a beautiful, sympathetic character, and a proper namesake for Pilar Palette Wayne as opposed to Josie in *Pittsburgh* back in 1942, a shady lady played by Marlene Dietrich with his then wife Josephine Saenz Morrison's nickname. One might almost judge Duke's current marital condition by the screen character bearing his wife's name.

And Pilar had been a good wife. Determined to share his first love rather than become a rival, she accompanied him on most of his picture locations. She packed a lot of spunk in her five-foot-three, one-hundred-pound nicely proportioned body and, although sometimes location life was not exactly what a Peruvian senator's daughter was accustomed to, she managed to fit in and was a great comfort to the star.

She had taken great pride in redecorating their Encino home, replacing everything that reflected Chata's somewhat heavy antique taste by opting for an Early American motif. She was especially pleased with the master bedroom, described by *Photoplay* magazine: "It had been really modernized: (the bed featured) armrests on the sides which could be raised or lowered; a cigarette compartment for him; a pulldown book rack; a control panel for television, radio, several telephone lines—by just flicking a switch you could turn on the lights downstairs or even open the front gate; a slide-out backgammon tray fitted into the headboard."

She showed that she was John Wayne's kind of woman when

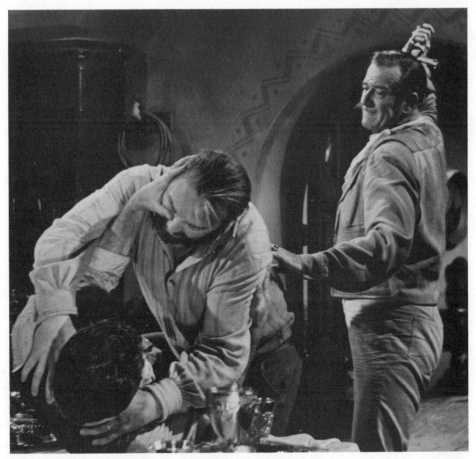

An unusual photograph showing the big star about to hit a man from behind while coming to Stuart Whitman's aid.

THE COMANCHEROS had an attractive, sexy brunette named Pilar in its cast. Here is the real life Pilar, the third Mrs. Wayne, with children Aissa, Marisa, and John Ethan. The elephant, we are assured, has no political significance.

Aissa was just two years old and her husband was in Japan on location filming *The Barbarian and the Geisha* in 1958. Just a month before she planned to join Duke, she awoke to the smell of smoke. Grabbing Aissa, she roused the servants and ran downstairs. When the fire department arrived, they found her gamely battling the spreading flames with a fire extinguisher. The second floor was practically destroyed, but she and the Peruvian servants had contained the flames long enough to save the rest of the house.

Wayne continues the gradual transformation he began in *She Wore a Yellow Ribbon*. No longer the dashing young lead, he is content to let Paul Regret win Pilar, and watches their love deepen with an avuncular understanding that adds to the depth of his still developing screen character. Actually the star was reversing the usual procedure, he was displaying more virility in his real than in his film life. Cast in the picture were Pat Wayne, a son by his first marriage, and Aissa Wayne, a daughter by his third. He may have been aging gracefully on the screen but he was giving it the old John Wayne tall-in-the-saddle treatment at home.

His next picture, *The Man Who Shot Liberty Valance*, saw him face an acting challenge in the modestly received John Ford production. Taking second billing to James Stewart, he was confronted with a very strong performance by Lee Marvin as Liberty Valance, as well as veteran scene-stealers such as Edmond O'Brien, Andy Devine, John Carradine, Lee Van Cleef, and Strother Martin.

Perhaps nothing reveals the thinking professional better than Wayne's post-production comments about the movie. "Well," he reminisced, "Liberty Valance was a tough assignment for me because, dammit, Ford had Jimmy for the shit-kicking humor; he had the Irishman, O'Brien, for the sophisticated humor; and he had that great heavy, Lee Marvin. Christ there was no place for me!

"I just had to wander around in that son-of-a-bitch and try to make a part for myself, and he (Ford) let me, too. I mean he just, goddammit, he forgot I was around. So he made it kind of rough on me."

That "Ford forgot I was around" is about the highest tribute an actor could hope for; it wasn't literally true, of course, but it does indicate the director's complete trust in the man he had to bully toward success in *Stagecoach*.

Wayne would take things from Ford that the star would never have tolerated from another director. Once, when Ford had sworn off liquor and Wayne was a star, the actor went on one of his relaxing sprees on location. The director stumbled across half his next day's cast roary-eyed drunk, with his star sitting in regal attendance. Irritated, Ford told Wayne: "Act your age. You're not a prop boy any more. Go to bed." The big man did just that.

Screen violence continued to escalate and in *The Man Who Shot Liberty Valance*, Wayne, who has just killed bad guy Valance, is forced to deal with some of his followers. In the ensuing melee he, among other mayhem, kicks Floyd (played by Strother Martin) in the face. Later, Martin talked about working with Wayne.

"I think," Martin said, "Duke respects hard work, especially in action scenes—and I'm sure he got his from John Ford. He's ready to bust his ass. And he expects everybody else to bust his ass. That's where you get in trouble with Duke, if you try to loaf through something."

*"All you gotta have in a John Wayne
is a hoity-toity dame
with big tits." —James Grant*

COMEDY

Who else would anyone cast as a stubborn, self-made cattle king named George Washington McLintock? He has a town named after him, a wife (Maureen O'Hara) who suspects he's been playing around and leaves him only to learn that he has hired Yvonne De Carlo as his "housekeeper." Although the plot sounds uncomfortably true to life, Wayne shows that he can play it for laughs under Victor McLaglen's son Andrew's first big-budget feature direction.

The picture is best remembered for a mud-fight scene employing well over a hundred extras and stunt men, but it contained a few references that tied in with Wayne's political philosophy. The inept territorial governor, Cuthbert H. Humphrey, had to be fictionally related to the late Minnesota senator whose liberal views conflicted with Wayne's own. Jerry Van Dyke has a small part that has him label McLintock a "reactionary" which is defined as "anyone who sells for a profit."

McLintock! provides us with yet another interesting

As MCLINTOCK! Duke is about literally to fall (down stairs)
for his "housekeeper" Yvonne De Carlo. The 1963 script
takes a few jabs at a prominent political leader.

background glimpse of John Wayne, the professional, making it
all look easy. Maureen O'Hara, who always worked well with him
in their pictures, tells of an incident during the shooting.

"He didn't like the way I was doing a scene," she recalls, "and
he said angrily, 'C'mon Maureen, get going. This is your scene.'

"I said I was trying to go fifty-fifty. 'Fifty-fifty, hell,' he said. 'It's
your scene, take it.' Then, he added under his breath, 'If you can.' "

As he gained control over the pictures in which he appeared
John Wayne began to rely more and more on family and old
friends for casting and technical help. On *McLintock!* his brother
Robert E. Morrison was the production supervisor, son Michael
Wayne was producer, son Patrick Wayne had a part as did daugh-
ter Aissa.

Pilar's role as a companion, as well as wife and lover, was
never more apparent than on *The Alamo*. She brought him a

*With Rita Hayworth in CIRCUS WORLD (1964). More than
just "a hoity-toity dame with big tits."*

reassurance he hadn't had with his first wives, a reason to *want* to return to his quarters after a day's shooting. He would tell Laurence Harvey that he looked forward to a hot bath, to rehashing the day with "my wife" before grabbing a quick dinner, and planning the camera setups to catch the early morning light. For the first time in his life John Wayne had found a companion in addition to a bedmate.

Not only was Pilar beautiful, her long dark hair and large, brown eyes perfectly complemented her flawless skin, but she was smart. She understood her husband's pride in his family and, perhaps against her better judgment, knew that when he wanted to cast four-year-old Aissa in the picture, she would do well to accede. So still another second generation Wayne made her acting debut as the daughter of an aide to Laurence Harvey's Colonel Travis; Wayne directed her scene with surprising tenderness and restraint.

His perhaps favorite cinematographer William H. Clothier, who had worked on many of the Ford movies, filmed the picture; Cliff Lyons who staged the impressive battle stunts on *The Alamo* staged the fight sequences; Chuck Roberson, the latter-day Yakima Canutt, had a small acting role; and the picture was written by James Edward Grant.

His loyalty to old friends made the circumstances surrounding his next picture *Circus World* (originally titled *The Magnificent Showman*), released in 1964, especially difficult. For the first time in their eighteen-year professional and close personal relationship, Duke Wayne did not back Jimmy Grant's play.

Wayne had first met Grant through Robert Fellows, the star's future partner in Wayne-Fellows Productions, in 1946. Grant had written *Angel and the Badman*; from then on the writer became Wayne's drinking companion and personal script writer. Grant, as we have seen, wrote some good as well as bad pictures; tended, especially when he was drinking, to throw his weight around as Duke's surrogate. He did it once too often on *Circus World*.

The picture was to be filmed in Spain; while Wayne cruised the Mediterranean on his yacht *The Wild Goose*, director Frank Capra worked on the script in Madrid. As had happened so many times before, Jimmy Grant showed up to rewrite the dialogue for Wayne, but Capra wasn't having any; the director quit, and after one script had been turned down by Duke who put in briefly at Lisbon to read it, Henry Hathaway took over as director, kicked Grant out of Spain, and hired Ben Hecht to rewrite the material.

Rumor had it that Wayne was cruising around knowing that the picture was hung up, feeling that the longer he stayed on the water the better terms he would get. Whatever the reason for his absence, when told that Capra had quit, and that Grant's presence was jeopardizing the project, the star agreed that Jimmy Grant must go. Grant died two years later of cancer without ever again writing a Wayne picture.

The story behind the CIRCUS WORLD camera was more startling than his fall here with Claudia Cardinale.

In his biography *Name Above The Title*, Capra tells us that "When you took on Wayne you took on a small empire," and recalls the circumstances surrounding his leaving *Circus World*. When Grant showed up in Madrid, the writer came right to the point.

"You're outta your mind, Capra," said Grant. "No use writing anything till Wayne gets here. Duke makes his own pictures, now. So relax, fella. When he gets here, he and I will knock you out a screenplay in a week. All you gotta have in a John Wayne is a hoity-toity dame with big tits that Duke can throw over his knee and spank, and a collection of jerks he can smash in the face every five minutes. In between you fill in with gags, flags and chases. That's all you need. His fans eat it up . . ."

Well, circus owner Matt Masters as played by Wayne had two ladies who at least partially matched Grant's unchivalrous description. Claudia Cardinale and Rita Hayworth play daughter and mother while John Smith provides the fourth romantic link. The plot is quite rudimentary, concerning Masters' loss of his circus and his efforts to put together a new one. It is the star's second circus picture (*Three Texas Steers* was the other in 1938) and, like the first, ends up in a shakily motivated big-top blaze that gives Duke a chance for some fire-fighting heroics.

The background story of *Circus World* adds a little more to our knowledge of John Wayne. If in fact he was cruising around on *The Wild Goose* to up the ante on a film that depended on his participation, we catch a glimpse of the same shrewd bargainer we saw assuring himself protection when he made *Reap The Wild Wind* for Cecil B. DeMille. And his permitting Hathaway to get rid of Jimmy Grant involves that same kind of difficult, no doubt, but hard professional decision when his vital interests are affected.

That yacht, by the way, gets around. Just recently with Wayne not on board, it was seized by the Royal Canadian Mounted Police for a violation of Canadian liquor laws. As reported by Radio Station CFRB in Toronto, Wayne's Captain Bert Minshall, after pointing out that the star had been bringing the boat into Canadian waters for over fifteen years, said that the owner was mighty upset by the seizure of twenty cases of bourbon bearing the personalized John Wayne label, and their subsequently being flushed down the drain of a local Mountie outpost.

CIRCUS WORLD's first director Frank Capra called him
a "small empire." Here are four reasons why.

"I'm not going to repeat what he said—it just wouldn't make good print," Captain Minshall said. "He wanted to go after the head honcho right away." The incident, largely unreported in the United States, was pure John Wayne: One can imagine him strapping on his gun belt, facing down a Mountie or two, and striding into the Prime Minister's office in the capital, Ottawa. I'm sure that every Wayne fan can supply his own version of the opening line of dialogue.

"I come for my booze," suggests itself.

Patricia Neal is the nurse in IN HARM'S WAY. Wayne holds an ever-present cigarette just weeks before being operated on for lung cancer after the picture's completion in 1964.

"I adored him."
— Patricia Neal

CANCER

Some industry people felt that when the freewheeling John Wayne met the disciplinarian Otto Preminger directing *In Harm's Way*, the picture's title would prove prophetic. But everything turned out well between the two men, although the 1965 film was not generally liked by the public. The story involved two naval officers—the other was Kirk Douglas—and how their different characters react to the stress of war and personal problems immediately following Pearl Harbor. The two stars' styles complement one another, their scenes together making for good theater. Patricia Neal played a Navy nurse providing the female interest.

Someone must have thought that Wayne hobbling around with two canes on a carrier flight deck in *The Wings of Eagles* looked suitably noble because they really roughed him up in this script. After having one ship torpedoed from under him, and suffering a fractured arm, he returns to duty, has another ship blown away, is knocked into a three-week coma, and wakes up with one leg amputated.

Wayne later had his own theory about the picture's disappointing reception at the box office. He felt that Preminger relied too heavily on what he termed "those goddam miniatures"—tiny mock-ups of ships supposedly in fleet action on the high seas, but filmed in a swimming-pool-sized studio tank. Which is a fine money and labor-saving device if they don't look like toys on the big screen.

The star put to rest any rumors about conflict between himself and the director. "He had my respect," Wayne told an interviewer, "and I had his respect. He is terribly hard on the crew, and he's terribly hard on people he thinks are sloughing off. But this is a thing I can understand because I've been there . . . I came ready and that he appreciated. I was usually there ahead of him on the set, and he couldn't believe that."

Is Wayne hard to work with? Pat Neal answered that very simply. "I adored him," she said.

After the principal photography of *In Harm's Way* was completed in 1964, John Wayne learned that he had cancer of the lung.

His wife Pilar had a great deal to do with that discovery. By now Aissa was eight years old and their second child, John Ethan, was two. She watched with growing concern as their father coughed repeatedly, bringing up blood-flecked phlegm. On location in Hawaii for *In Harm's Way*, he returned to their hotel suite at the end of the day breathing heavily and barely able to cross the room without sitting down to rest. Only his massive willpower kept him going on the picture, but when he told her that any medical examination would have to wait until he fulfilled his next picture commitment on *The Sons of Katie Elder*, she uncharacteristically defied him.

At her urging, sons Pat and Mike and his brother Bob Morrison arranged to have him check into the Scripps Clinic at La Jolla, California for a five-day series of tests. He returned home and told Pilar; she took it the way she knew he wanted: No tears, no hysteria although she must have been torn up inside. Her husband was admitted to Good Samaritan Hospital in Los Angeles on September 16, 1964; his left lung and two ribs were removed the following morning. After complications in the recovery room, he was operated on again and a small portion of his right lung excised.

When the time came to go home, he was taken to the ground

*Leaving Good Samaritan Hospital in Los Angeles, Oct. 7, 1964
with Pilar after two successful lung operations.*

*With Earl Holliman, left, and Dean Martin in THE SONS OF
KATIE ELDER (1965). Made scarcely three months after his
hospital release, the picture gave notice to a legion
of fans that cancer could be overcome.*

floor in a wheelchair but insisted on getting to his feet, with Pilar
helping steady him, to walk through the door to meet the waiting
press.

At first the Batjac brigade tried to conceal the seriousness of the
star's condition. He had "respiratory problems" that graduated to a
"chest tumor"; the day he was released from the hospital on October 7, 1964, the Associated Press reported that he had been operated on for a lung abscess and, interestingly, an old ankle injury.
(Would the famous Wayne walk be altered? It would not.)

After a cruise down the Mexican coast on *The Wild Goose*,
Wayne, remarkably recovered, held a press conference to tell the
world that he had indeed had cancer but that he had "licked the
Big C." He did this against the advice of his business associates.

"They told me," he revealed to the assembled media, "to with-hold my cancer operation from the public because it would hurt my image."

Just the opposite happened. Big Duke had licked Big C., and his fans loved him for it. He advised them to have regular check-ups; not only that, wonder of wonders, he admitted he had "prayed to God" prior to the operation. Wayne's selfless decision to use his experience to give courage to others had resulted in unanticipated public relations dividends.

Oh, Duke had one other announcement at that press confer-ence: He would be leaving for Mexico in one month to begin filming *The Sons of Katie Elder*. That simple, incredible an-nouncement put cancer in an entirely new perspective for mil-lions of people. Cancer had interrupted Duke's schedule for a couple of months, and that was it; he was back living a normal life, just like anyone else.

Well, not quite like anyone else. The *Sons of Katie Elder* was a brawling, gunfighting, hard-riding action movie, and Wayne was right in the middle of it all incurring, reports had it, a powerful thirst in the process. Anyone who had four offspring like Katie Elder's was probably doomed to a sad life: Wayne as John, a gunfighter; Dean Martin as Tom, a cardsharp living by his wits; Earl Holliman as the obsessively withdrawn Matt and—inevitably—young Bud, played by Michael Anderson, Jr., who somehow manages to be a normal kid wanting, of all things, to further his education.

The sons set out to get the man who killed their father, do so, and provide us with some great action in the process. Martin is especially good, showing us that his role in *Rio Bravo* was no fluke, and Holliman provides the kind of steady, clearly defined performance that has had him, like Wayne, taken for granted by both the audience and his peers in the course of a truly distin-guished career.

The Sons of Katie Elder was exactly the kind of picture Wayne should have made following his cancer operations. It was a statement, an encouragement to everyone for whom the disease had taken on mythical proportions. A living legend, a man we could see and touch, had once again come through for us, facing up to the enemy and flattening him like any other bad guy.

*CAST A GIANT SHADOW (1966) linked German concentration
camps with the founding of Israel. Here Kirk Douglas
shows Dachau to his superior officer.*

"Due process out here is a bullet."
— line of dialogue

23.
THE GREEN BERETS

Cast A Giant Shadow cast an exceedingly small shadow at the box office. A message picture, it tied the German concentration camps in with the emerging Jewish state as Kirk Douglas played real-life Colonel David "Mickey" Marcus, a soldier who helped shape the fledgling Israeli Army. The chemistry that worked so well in *In Harm's Way* between Wayne and Douglas—one stolid and determined, the other impulsive and aggressive—failed to repeat itself, mostly because Wayne had such a relatively minor role. It was a 1966 film made before its time and despite Duke's (and Frank Sinatra's) appearances to hype theater attendance the picture was not strong enough to make it as entertainment.

Undaunted, Universal cast Wayne and Douglas together the following year in *The War Wagon* with not much better results.

Bruce Cabot is the evil character who has Wayne put in jail on a false charge after cheating him out of his land and mining his gold. As though that isn't enough to dump on our hero, Cabot hires Kirk Douglas to gun Wayne down. Instead Wayne talks Douglas into helping him hijack the war wagon, an armored coach in which Cabot transports his ill-gotten gains.

The two conspirators really don't trust one another but the fine comedic interplay between Stuart Whitman and Wayne in *The Comancheros* never materializes here despite scenes like those that have Wayne and Douglas ready to hit the sack wearing long johns and gun belts.

Sometimes seemingly small occurrences can become major distractions; in this case, the casting of Howard Keel as Levi

Douglas played real life Colonel David "Mickey" Marcus in a message film made ahead of its time.

*Robert Walker is either offering a drink or handing
over some explosive in THE WAR WAGON, released in 1967.
Duke seems pleased either way.*

Walking Bear, a friendly Indian from—we must presume—
Oklahoma!, more than made up for the conscious humor that
didn't quite come off. Assisted by Robert Walker and Keenan
Wynn, the gold is successfully intercepted only, in turn, to be
stolen by a band of marauding Indians. Douglas plays everything
too compulsively to project the subtleties of a half-humorous
mutual distrust, given Wayne's own broad-brush characterization. It was a pleasant enough picture that didn't quite work out.

El Dorado, made next, demonstrated two things: John
Wayne's fictional character had a built-in license literally to
commit murder, and the gradual-aging process—casting him as
an older, less assured, slower reacting gunfighter—could be carried too far.

This picture was the second of three Howard Hawks westerns;

the third would be *Rio Lobo*. Here we have Robert Mitchum in the *Rio Bravo* Dean Martin role complete with a booze problem, James Caan as yet another Billy-the-Kid type and Charlene Holt in Angie Dickinson's role. There is little question but that both Hawks and Wayne considered it a sequel to *Rio Bravo*. The plot, sheriff's good-guy gunfighters against land baron's bad-guy gunfighters, was essentially the same. When Hawks first told Wayne that he wanted him for the new western, the star asked, "Do I get to play the drunk this time?"

Prior to *Red River* back in 1948, Hawks had told Duke, "If you can make two good scenes and not annoy the audience for the rest of the film, you'll be a star." Now Wayne asked the director, "Is this one of those not-annoy-the-audience things?"

Well, Wayne didn't annoy the audience, but considering who he was, and in his favorite western setting, he came quite close. It certainly wasn't all his fault. In addition to casting him as an aging gunfighter, the script has him shot twice, the first time partially paralyzing him for short periods (he falls down a lot), and the second time putting him on crutches. It strains even John Wayne-anesthetized credulity to have him become unexpectedly immobilized during key action scenes, on one occasion actually having to crawl behind a rock to hide. The second element that makes this an iffy Wayne western is the fact that he gets away with murder. Christopher George is a rival gunman who, as a "professional courtesy" stops a proposed ambush of Wayne only to be tricked and coldly shot down, with his hands empty, by Wayne using a rifle at close range.

As George lies dying he protests, "You didn't even give me a chance." To which Wayne replies, "You're too good to give a chance to." Now, this is something different than a shoot-out, or even gunning someone down when he has taken his best shot, literally and figuratively, at you; this was a cold-blooded killing by a man who couldn't have won a face-to-face showdown. Wayne brings it off, but barely. There is just that flicker of hesitation, of uncertainty when you see George (who does an excellent job) shot. Did Wayne's character behave criminally or, perhaps even worse, ignobly?

Wayne must have sensed it, too, because he never repeated the mistake.

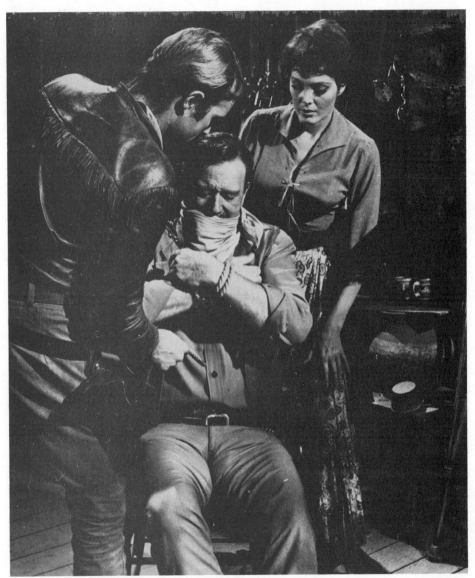

With a concerned Charlene Holt in EL DORADO (1967). Does even John Wayne have a license to commit murder?

*Robert Mitchum, playing a drunk, has one of his funniest roles in
EL DORADO. This sequence required great timing by both stars.*

A little cheesecake supplied by Charlene Holt in
any young actress's dream situation.

Never was the Sam Goldwyn observation, "If you have a message, send it Western Union," more valid than in *The Green Berets* produced and co-directed by its star, John Wayne. He spoke of Americanism in *The Alamo* and didn't make a dime; he did it again in *The Green Berets* and made money, but invoked the wrath of even those who usually liked what he did on the screen. In *Big Jim McLain* made in 1952, critics took potshots at Duke for his unabashed deification of the House Un-American Activities Committee; in *The Green Berets* they riddled him with machine gun fire for his espousal of a generally unpopular war.

Bob Thomas of the Associated Press asked Wayne about his motives in making the picture. "Nobody's enjoying this war but it happens to be necessary," Wayne replied. "If we hadn't gone into Vietnam, Indonesia wouldn't have been encouraged to fight the Communists in their country. Thailand, which is the heart of the rice country in Southeast Asia, would have fallen to the Communists . . . Besides, we gave our word."

We gave our word. A line from a dozen John Wayne pictures that is so eloquent in its brevity. And in the light of current developments in Cambodia and Thailand, Wayne's evaluation doesn't appear quite so simplistic. But in 1968 even respected film critics looked right past the picture and used it to berate John Wayne.

Renata Adler wrote in the *New York Times*: "*The Green Berets* is a film so unspeakable, so stupid, so rotten and false in every detail that it passes through being fun, through being funny, through being camp, through everything . . . It is vile and insane. On top of that, it is dull."

The lady's heart doth rule her head. It certainly wasn't a dull picture, and packed theaters made it one of the star's highest grossers, ever. It had great action scenes, and the same one-sided philosophy that was characteristic of all World War II movies. Admittedly a line like, "Due process out here is a bullet," causes any thinking person to cringe, but to a lot of Americans the Communists *were* the bad guys. But not, according to Duke, to a certain segment of the press.

"That little clique back there in the East," he told a *Chicago Sun-Times* interviewer, "have taken great personal satisfaction in reviewing my politics instead of my pictures. And they've drawn up a caricature of me."

The very existence of a caricature implies something or someone to be caricatured in the first place. Although in some cases critics reviewed the man rather than the picture, it should be pointed out that his very strength lies in the honesty of his screen portrayals, an honesty that stems from his own personality. If that honesty sometimes gets him into trouble, then that is a price that must be paid.

THE GREEN BERETS made money in 1968, but tried the patience of many fans. Bruce Cabot on the extreme left sits next to the late Jack Soo, who became a television personality on the BARNEY MILLER show. The girl is Irene Tsu.

One of the few times he permits another male to stand taller than himself in a still photograph. A proud father with sons Patrick (left) and Michael on the set of THE GREEN BERETS.

24.
AN ACADEMY AWARD

John Wayne's first picture in 1969, *Hellfighters*, is largely, and deservedly overshadowed in the public's memory by his second, *True Grit*.

Even without *True Grit* and Wayne's Academy Award, *Hellfighters*, based on the real-life exploits of oil well fire fighter Red Adair, remains less than memorable. Surrounding himself with some of his favorite people, director Andrew McLaglen, cinematographer William Clothier, stunt man and stand-in Chuck Roberson, writer Clair Huffaker, and actor Bruce Cabot, didn't help Duke very much.

A picture about a man who fights oil well fires is great when he's actually fighting the fires (and Wayne seemed to be in the thick of those action scenes), but without a meaningful story line the rest of it tends to fall flat. Writer Huffaker (who likes to name his characters Lomax, Jay C. Flippen here and Kirk Douglas in *The War Wagon*) had trouble with his characterizations and despite the presence of Katharine Ross, a new star just risen from *The Graduate*, and the always dependable Vera Miles we can't get too excited about the story.

Then he made *True Grit*, the story of a cantankerous, drunken, courageous, yet kindly U.S. Marshal—a character that it would seem Wayne had been building toward for forty years. Directed by Henry Hathaway who first directed the star in *The Shepherd of the Hills* in 1941, the film has a standard John Wayne plot as a young girl, Kim Darby, hires a gunman, John Wayne, who happens to be on the side of the law, to bring Jeff Corey, her father's murderer, to justice.

Despite the curious casting of balladeer Glen Campbell as a Texas Ranger with the unlikely name of La Boeuf (a name that may be translated idiomatically as "Meat"—is someone putting us on?), the picture works. Wayne plays his age, and, according to his own earlier quote, his disposition—displaying on the screen his real-life ability to cut through all the horseshit.

The best remembered scene evolves when he is bragging to Kim Darby, who has insisted on tagging along with Wayne and Campbell in search of the killer, how, as a younger man, he had singlehandedly charged whole gangs of outlaws and sent them sprawling. The trio comes face to face with notorious outlaw Robert Duvall and some of his top guns. Duvall pays him the compliment of suggesting they each mind their own business, but Wayne, flushed from his recounting of his exploits and into the sauce, challenges the gunslinger; Duvall disgustedly refers to him as "a one-eyed fat man."

Enraged, Wayne takes his horse's reins in his teeth, and with a Winchester in one hand and a six-shooter in the other, spurs his horse forward yelling to the outlaw to "Fill your hand, you son-of-a-bitch." He wins the fight with an assist from Campbell and goes on to find and dispatch Jeff Corey. A subplot has Kim Darby bitten by a snake; Wayne commandeers a wagon at gunpoint to rush her to town in time to save her life.

It was a bravura performance and mercifully eased the memory of *The Green Berets* in most critics' minds.

William Wolf of *Cue* magazine wrote, "When the John Wayne

retrospectives are in full swing, this will loom as one of his finest movie triumphs."

The *New York Times* reviewer Vincent Canby hailed the film as "major entertainment" and chose it as one of the year's ten best films.

Explosive action in HELLFIGHTERS (1969) is the key to this oil well fire fighter story. But interest dies with the flames.

An Academy Award for portraying "A mean, tough, old son-of-a-bitch, just like me," was the star's description of his peers' response to TRUE GRIT in 1969.

Andrew Sarris said it for many fans, "And there is talk of an Oscar for Wayne after forty years of movie acting and after thirty years of damn good movie acting . . . Ironically, Wayne has become a legend by not being legendary. He has dominated the screen even when he has not been written in as the dominant character."

And so on April 14, 1970 at the Dorothy Chandler Pavilion in the Los Angeles Music Center complex, Reuben J. "Rooster" Cogburn, aka John Wayne, received both an Academy Award and, a Hollywood rarity, a truly spontaneous ovation.

Wayne had come over to Los Angeles from location in Arizona where he was making *Rio Lobo*, the last of the Howard Hawks western trilogy. True to his work ethic (and showing true grit after partying all night) he reported back to location early next morning to find everyone wearing a "Rooster" eyepatch, even his horse! One wonders which tribute touched him more.

*Duke in action as CHISUM in 1970. Modern screen
brawling techniques owe a great deal to his early experiments
with stunt man Yakima Canutt.*

"Don't ever get tough, because Wayne will blow you right off the screen." — Howard Hawks

25.
JOHN ETHAN WAYNE

As professional writers never tire of pointing out, you can have a good director, in this case Andrew McLaglen, a good cinematographer, William Clothier, a hell of a star, John Wayne, but if the writing is weak the picture probably will be flawed. What makes writers somewhat paranoid is that the story in question is most often the work of an experienced colleague.

Chisum, an account of the Lincoln County cattle war, proves the writers' point. It's essentially about two people, John Simpson Chisum (Wayne) a cattle baron, and nineteen-year-old William Bonney (played by Geoffrey Deuel) who, as Billy the Kid, gained wide notoriety as a quick-draw, hot-tempered deadly killer. Some western historians refer to Billy as a true psychotic, and contemporary photos show him as a squinty-eyed, pimpled little guy whom a sane man wouldn't turn his back on. Billy was hired by rich, ruthless landowners to kill men, which he did with efficiency and apparent relish.

In *Chisum*, Billy's temper is treated as a growing pain by an indulgent, somewhat paternal Chisum. The Kid emerges as a shy, likable lad who is loyal to his friends (*naturally* he wants to avenge the death of his first boss, Patrick Knowles). A more strongly drawn character might have challenged Duke for control of the picture but such was not the case. About all we have as a remembered keepsake is a shoot-out between Wayne and some Mexican cattle thieves plus a fine brawl between Wayne and Forrest Tucker. Tucker does the best he can as a businessman with evil intentions of bankrupting the town and buying it back at his price.

Rio Lobo, for Howard Hawks, has Wayne replaying his role in *Rio Bravo* with considerably less enthusiasm than he showed

RIO LOBO (1970), the last of director Howard Hawks's western trilogy, finds the star first as a Union officer . . .

. . . then in Confederate uniform. "Don't ever get tough,"
Hawks advised a young actor, "because Wayne will
blow you right off the screen."

when, in *Rio Bravo*, he first replayed his role in *El Dorado*. The
message of this story about a Union colonel during the Civil War
pursuing some Confederate troops who have stolen a gold ship-
ment and killed an officer friend of his is . . . enough is enough.

Not even Howard Hawks, with Wayne and stalwarts like Jack
Elam, and a second-unit action camera directed by Yakima
Canutt, can breathe much life into the same plot and characters a
third time around. Jennifer O'Neill, possibly because of the direction, does not show what the future has in store for her as an
actress, but Victor French, later to achieve television stardom as
the southern sheriff in the television comedy *Carter Country*, acquits himself very well as Ketcham, the man Wayne is chasing.

Director Hawks's instructions to young actor Jorge Rivero
who plays a Confederate soldier, tell us all there is to know about

187

the subject of this book. "Don't ever get tough," Hawks advised, "because Wayne will blow you right off the screen—your only chance is to be quieter than he is." That's another version of "steal the scene, if you can." Rivero, who gives a very low-key performance, had the good sense not to try.

Wayne appears as both a Union and a Confederate officer as the film progresses, with the Confederate uniform much the scruffier, to show who the good guys are. The Wayne acting dynasty continues in *Rio Lobo* with John Ethan Wayne, Pilar's son, making a screen appearance.

Matter of fact, *Big Jake*, Wayne's initial 1971 release, casts young John Ethan in a role that speaks volumes for both his dad's

That's number two son Patrick Wayne on the ground for daring to point a gun at BIG JAKE as Maureen O'Hara watches in the 1971 release.

personal and professional life. It features the young man's first screen credit; he plays Little Jack McCandles, the grandson of Big Jacob McCandles played by John Wayne! Surely a first; the star permitting his son to appear as his grandson on screen tells us two things: Wayne isn't afraid to acknowledge his on-screen aging but, mister, yuh better not confuse that with any slowing down in the virility department in real life.

Big Jake McCandles, who like George Washington McLintock, has a town named after him, and a disillusioned wife (she suspects in both pictures that he fools around) played by Maureen O'Hara, is after the men who raided his spread and kidnapped his grandson. Richard Boone, a television star as the man who has gun, will travel, plays the leader of the renegade band very convincingly and Patrick Wayne (real life number two son) and Chris Mitchum (star Robert's offspring) do well as Wayne's fictional sons.

But it's John Ethan who shows he's a real chip off the old block by plugging one of the bad guys with a small derringer pistol and, in typical Wayne fashion, bringing off what might charitably be called an improbable sequence with professional aplomb. John Ethan's older sister Aissa has appeared briefly in films but his younger sister Marisa has not.

Nothing better illustrates the wondrous behind-the-camera fashionings of Hollywood folklore than an event that took place shortly after *Rio Lobo*. John Wayne was about to have a theater named after him at Knott's Berry Farm, a sprawling complex of shops and entertainment facilities set on old-fashioned western streets in Buena Park, a half-hour freeway ride from Los Angeles. Broadway super stars have traditionally been honored by having legitimate theaters renamed for them, but this was an unusual event. The theater was brand new, a spacious 2000-seater, featuring a stage that converted easily for ice shows, and a cascading column of water that flowed down from the proscenium arch in place of the traditional curtain.

Walter Knott, the Farm's founder and long-time Wayne personal friend and business associate, pulled out all the publicity stops as Wayne, accompanied by John Ethan, officially declared the John Wayne Theater open for everything from Broadway musicals to laser-augmented three-dimensional photo projection. The result was a textbook Hollywood press triumph.

*Washing off the trail dust in this John Wayne
version of a magazine centerfold nude.*

Wayne's presence and name gave the theater instant national recognition; Wayne himself gained the added prestige of lending his name to the theater. Since Walter Knott and Wayne saw eye-to-eye politically the signal went out to the faithful, while the liberals could eat their hearts out; a future star, single-shot John Ethan Wayne, was given exposure that established actors would envy; and, to top it all off, Duke had himself photographed with Knott resident Indian Chief White Eagle, slowing the tempo of

Congratulating his son John Ethan on his first screen credit as the star's fictional grandson in BIG JAKE. Ethan's sister Aissa also had a small role.

*John Ethan on his first full-fledged publicity outing following his film
debut. Here with his dad, Chief White Eagle, and old friend Walter Knott
at the christening of the John Wayne Theater in California.*

the American Indian Movement war dance. And all in the name of
better entertainment for the public.

About this time a strain was beginning to show in the star's
personal life, a strain that would not affect his or Pilar's relationship with their children. More and more, with the death of old
buddies like Yak Canutt, Ward Bond, and Victor McLaglen, the
star was feeling a sense of loss that even she could not assuage.
His love for her had never been questioned by either of them,
indeed would not be questioned when they finally separated.

After moving into their beautiful Newport Beach home Pilar became interested in tennis, and Wayne immediately ordered the construction of "Pilar's tennis courts," even confiding that he might well take up the game himself. But he seemed determined to stave off old age or, rather, the image of old age that he had cultivated in those later westerns. He appeared in cops-and-robbers pictures like *Cahill, United States Marshal, McQ*, and *Brannigan*, pictures that, it was said, Pilar thought were harmful to his career and to him personally, exhausting his physical resources when he should have been at home with his growing family.

She had softened him, made him more empathetic of others' problems, and brought a new sense of values to his personal relationships. Ironically some critics blamed this new humaneness for the failure of the *Green Berets*, claiming that he could no longer project the unyielding toughness needed for that kind of role. It was a harsh analysis, but the suggestion that he had gone soft angered him and he set out to prove on the screen that he was as good, or as bad, as ever.

The trophy room of the John Wayne Theater containing memorabilia from the star's major motion pictures.

But he was not the same man, and Pilar, who saw that she, like Josie and Chata before her, was fighting a losing battle, surrendered to the one mistress she could not defeat, his career. They separated in 1973 with neither willing to discuss the circumstances with the press. United by a common love for their children and his twenty-one grandchildren, they lived apart with, wonder of wonders, Pilar's privacy respected by the media. When asked if he would ever remarry Wayne replied, "Three strikes and you're out," and that's the way it has remained.

"Wayne is a lovely man."
— Katharine Hepburn

26.
GROWING OLD

The fact that *The Cowboys*, Wayne's only picture released in 1972, was booked into Radio City Music Hall in New York, then removed before its allotted run because of poor attendance is not, in itself, that significant. Radio City had trouble drawing an audience for almost any motion picture (it was just recently saved from extinction by the last-minute efforts of concerned New Yorkers).

The picture's first-run failure does, however, invite some speculation regarding John Wayne, the actor and the man. How long, the question begs to be asked, can Duke go on growing older on the screen? In his next three pictures, all westerns, he emphasized his characters' increasing years. Then, playing a cop for the first time in *McQ* in 1974 he suddenly, and not too successfully, goes modern on us, keeping the aging process in check.

*One of the things that Duke does best: Flattening bad
guy Bruce Dern in THE COWBOYS (1972). The star's treasured
screen image may have slipped in this one.*

*Bridging the generation gap. Visiting on THE COWBOYS
set with its young director Mark Rydell and the
legendary John Ford seated in the car.*

The Cowboys has Wayne as an elderly rancher deserted by hired
hands lured by a gold rush, enlisting the aid of very young boys (one
of them John Carradine's son, Bob) in a cattle drive. The star
deserted his own Batjac spread and familiar list of supporting
actors for this one, relying on Mark Rydell, a young proponent of the
realism school of film, to produce and direct. It's a measure of
Wayne's professional objectivity that he could see the potential in
the story, and the fitness of a fresh group of talent to implement it.

Rydell, uncertain how the veteran conservative would take
direction from a relatively wet-behind-the-ears, avant-garde
whippersnapper, told David Castell in *Films Illustrated*: "We had
it quite clear from the start that I was producer and director. He

was delighted to surrender all managerial rights and be just an actor in this film. He was as happy as a twenty-year-old and called me 'Sir' right the way through shooting. Me! He's been a star for more years than I've been alive."

A seemingly ideal professional relationship, yet an incident on screen was damaging to Duke's image. After beating up bad guy Bruce Dern, thirty years his junior, in a grueling fistfight Wayne turns away from the prone man only to be shot in the back by Dern and killed. John Wayne, directed by Hawks or Ford or Wellman, would never have permitted the incident. Wayne would be a much better judge of men than that. In this case, continuity of character, the image that had become larger than

Another family film dynasty in the making? John Carradine watched his son Bob make his acting debut as one of THE COWBOYS.

*"I've got a saddle older than you are," Wayne tells
Ann-Margret in THE TRAIN ROBBERS (1973). Was it needless
emphasis on his obvious aging?*

This is the way we think of him at his best. But in
CAHILL: UNITED STATES MARSHAL he seemed again to be
stressing the vulnerability of his character.

life, was cavalierly cast aside in the interests of realism. Certainly it was realistic to suppose that Dern would shoot Wayne as soon as the star turned his back, but the classic screen John Wayne would never have put himself in that position.

In Wayne's next, *The Train Robbers*, he tells Ann-Margret "I've got a saddle older than you are," discouraging her amorous advances. Duke pushing a young doll away? In the same picture he confidently predicts that a group of pursuing gunmen will not fire on him and his pals, only to have them open up seconds later. This one was produced by Batjac so we can't suspect anyone's motives. It simply seems that Wayne and those advising him are infusing the role of an aging gunfighter-rancher-marshal with needless, and from the public's point of view, unacceptable senility. The irony of the usual order being reversed—Wayne very much in command in

A sudden switch to television-inspired cops-and-robbers in BRANNIGAN (1974), his only picture made in England. Not exactly John Wayne country.

private but seemingly losing a step or two fictionally—merely adds to the dismay of Duke's solid core of fans.

When, in *Cahill, United States Marshal*, he confronts a gang of badmen, and after conferring with their leader (played by Chuck Roberson), contemptuously rides through them without anyone so much as doubling their fists, we are being asked to accept unintended caricature. The discipline that kept John Wayne in character is being eroded; a deadly illness is accomplishing in his professional life what Big C could not do to his person: We begin to doubt the integrity of his fictional portrayals.

Those doubts are, if anything, accentuated by Wayne's next two films, *McQ* and *Brannigan*. He plays a modern, television-

He walks like John Wayne and he talks like John Wayne, but submachine guns and car chases are hard to get used to in McQ, another 1974 detective role.

If 12-year-old John Ethan, here visiting his dad
on location with McQ, keeps growing at his present pace
and can learn that Wayne walk . . .

*Time out in 1974 for a then rare television appearance,
and some good laughs, as he visited ultra-liberal Maude Findlay
on MAUDE, the popular CBS show that starred Beatrice Arthur.*

type cop in both; *Brannigan* is his only picture filmed in England
and, while it is impossible for him not to bring something to a
role, it is difficult for us to become accustomed to him handling
submachine guns and being involved in car chases. They just
didn't have those things in John Wayne country.

Now a Gatling gun is another matter. And that forerunner of
the modern machine gun is what John Wayne employs to get
Katharine Hepburn and himself out of a tight spot in *Rooster
Cogburn*. Released in 1975, this much admired picture seems to
muster all the legend's resources, bringing them into line for a
delightfully on-target characterization of the man from *True Grit*
who meets up with a minister's old maid daughter. Together they
conquer the elements, the bad guys, and the audiences' hearts, as
a pairing that nearly took place in *Hondo* in 1953 more than

fulfills our expectations.

Rooster Cogburn was, it now seems, a marvelous act that is proving hard to follow. Wayne tried it with *The Shootist* in 1976, co-starring James Stewart, Lauren Bacall, and, with a nod to the generation gap, Ron Howard. Despite the fact that Bacall looked ravishing, much more of a romantic possibility for Duke than was Hepburn, it was a picture about old men made by old men. Wayne was faced with the fact that a visibly aging westerner

Both Wayne and Katharine Hepburn had it all together for
ROOSTER COGBURN, the very well received 1975 sequel to TRUE
GRIT. Almost cast in HONDO in 1953, the famous actress waited
twenty-two years to appear with the star she called "a lovely man."

wearing a gun, riding a horse, and challenging man and nature—even if the rider was John Wayne—no longer had wide audience acceptance.

With James Cagney as a notable exception, big screen stars— especially male stars—find it hard to hang up their toupees. Ray Milland took his *off* and prolonged his career, but shattered the recollections of a host of admiring fans. After undergoing open heart surgery in 1978, Wayne, recuperating at his Newport Beach, California home, was quoted as saying that he would perform "as long as people like to watch me."

The basic premise of *The Shootist*—the story of an aging gun- fighter, played by Wayne, dying of cancer—led to a shocking real-life parallel when, in January 1979, the star was admitted to the U.C.L.A. Medical Center for what was described as a routine gall bladder operation; as routine as any surgery could be on a seventy-one-year-old man who had survived a bout with cancer and had recently undergone an open-heart operation.

Knowledgeable people greeted the announcement of the Duke's new ordeal with raised eyebrows. Why U.C.L.A.? Good Samaritan Hospital had been the choice for his first cancer oper- ation, and the gall bladder procedure was normally much less demanding than that. On the other hand, U.C.L.A. has a reputa- tion as a medical court of last resort, a complex of specialists who deal with only the gravest cases or those in which there is a suggestion of research that would break new medical ground.

On January 13 as the "routine" two to three hour operation stretched to an incredible nine hours on the table, nine hours with life support systems being monitored by teams of medical per- sonnel operating in shifts, it became clear that something was very much amiss. Even then, as they had done during the period of his first cancer operation and recovery, John Wayne's business associates and family—in reality almost one and the same— chose to mislead the public. This was done, according to one source close to the star's advisers, because any news of an illness that could possibly prove fatal, tended to bring all Wayne finan- cial activity to a halt.

A business whose raw material and product are consolidated in a single individual is notoriously vulnerable; long term advertis- ing contracts, future picture commitments, large bank loans

Twenty-one years after BLOOD ALLEY Lauren Bacall looked as ravishing as ever in THE SHOOTIST released in 1976.

whose collateral was named "Duke," future enterprises whose funding depended on the Wayne presence, these and many other facets of the one-man conglomerate had to be taken into account. So an eager, fearful public was told that a tumor, discovered during the operation, had necessitated removal of the entire stomach. Which was fine, as far as it went.

Wayne fans can be forgiven, however, if in hindsight they resent the further implication that their idol "except for minor complications involving a surgical scar infection" had been given a clean bill of health. After three days in the eleventh floor intensive care unit, a lengthy stay by any standards, he was moved into Room 951 which, with its decorator wallpaper, designer furniture, and original paintings hanging on the walls, looks more like a cheerful hotel suite than a hospital facility.

Meanwhile the Medical Center pathologists were analyzing tissue and confirming a condition that could be kept private only for a short while. The new diagnosis: Gastric carcinoma located in the lymph glands around the stomach. Called "one of the most lethal types of cancer," its location made it more than ninety percent certain that it had already spread by the time of the gall bladder operation.

John Wayne was told of the medical findings and of the dismaying prognosis: A high grade malignancy that might well limit his life to a few months. Chemotherapy, he was told, might help arrest the cancer's progress, a very big "might." And that would mean a continuing hospital stay, confined there possibly for the rest of his life with all the debilitating side effects of the severe treatment. Worst of all the star would be deprived of his dignity, something as we have learned, he prized very highly. So, with the full knowledge that he was quite probably signing his own death warrant, at 10:30 A.M. on Sunday, February 11, twenty-nine days after his operation John Wayne went home.

He went out a side door, in a wheelchair, protected by Medical Center security guards and his sons Pat, Mike, and John Ethan. Queen Elizabeth of Britain, Queen Juliana of the Netherlands, and actress Elizabeth Taylor were among those who had telephoned their good wishes. Thousands of cards and letters flowed into the Medical Center, and he took them home with him, a still defiant but much more appreciative man.

He had plans for the three children still at home, Aissa, 22, John Ethan, 17, and Marisa, 13: He hoped to use the force of his personality to help them with their futures. He wanted them to be examples of what young America stands for, as a counter to the dropped-out young people who used Vietnam as an excuse for indolence and sloth. As always, he was trying to serve his country the best way he knew how; it was a private goal that, like all his business enterprises, needed a fully functioning symbol to make it work.

No matter how that goal is eventually fulfilled, Duke can rest secure in the knowledge that he has given millions—a word

James Stewart had top billing in THE MAN WHO SHOT LIBERTY VALANCE in 1962. Fourteen years later the order is reversed in THE SHOOTIST, but the picture didn't quite catch on.

Recuperating at his home in Newport Beach, California in 1978 after open-heart surgery. He will perform "as long as people like to watch me."

casually employed in these days of billions terminology, but in reality a staggering number—of people great pleasure. He has annoyed, or even angered, a far smaller number.

Is John Wayne, as Joan Didion wrote in, *John Wayne: A Love Story*, someone "who determined forever the shape of certain of our dreams."? Or is he, as critic Manny Farber suggests, merely an actor whose "ignorant blustering" is not to be taken seriously?

If he is either of those, a little of both, or neither, he remains forever a part of the American ethos that will never be erased. He is here to stay, so much taken for granted that use of his name as a point of reference seems natural, and is immediately understood.

Syndicated sport columnist Jim Murray, commenting on the Yankees winning the 1978 World Series, wanted to stress that feat's inevitability. "They (the Yankees) won it in four straight (after the Dodgers had taken the first two games)," he wrote. "And the sun rises in the east and two-and-two make four and John Wayne is American . . ."

No better illustration is provided of the star's towering status as an indestructible synonym for the American way than a recent (1979) article in the *New York Times* dealing with the modern American Indians' struggle for power and identity. Writer Howell Raines quotes Peter MacDonald, chairman of the Navajo nation, on methods used to increase the various tribes' influence. "We used the same trick that John Wayne would use," MacDonald explained. "We circled the wagons. We circled the tribes and said, 'By golly . . . you're not going to deal just with the Crow or just with the Navajo or just with the Cheyenne. You've got to deal with the rest of us." At last the Duke seems to have had a hand in bringing the "elements of dignity and respect" he wanted so badly for those very same Indians who often verbally rode against him. The irony of their deliverance would not be lost on John Wayne.

Perhaps his *Rooster Cogburn* co-star said it best for the majority of present and future fans who will know him only as a screen legend. "Wayne is a lovely man," Katharine Hepburn said. "Warm-funny-bright-wild. And a damn good actor. He's just exactly what we've all adored . . . all these years. He's a hero. And he's ours."

Fair enough.

Filmography

HANGMAN'S HOUSE (1928)

Director: John Ford

Produced by: Fox

Starring: Victor McLaglen
June Collyer
with (uncredited) Duke Morrison as an extra

WORDS AND MUSIC (1929)

Director: James Tinling

Produced by: Fox

Starring: Lois Moran
David Percy
Helen Twelvetrees
with the role of Steve Donahue played by
Duke Morrison (his first screen credit)

SALUTE (1929)

Director: John Ford

Produced by: Fox

Starring: George O'Brien
Helen Chandler
with Duke Morrison and Ward Bond as
football players

MEN WITHOUT WOMEN (1930)

Director: John Ford

Produced by: Fox

Starring: Kenneth MacKenna
Frank Albertson
with Duke Morrison in a bit part

ROUGH ROMANCE (1930)

Director: A.F. Erickson

Produced by: Fox

Starring: George O'Brien
Helen Chandler
with Duke Morrison in a bit part

CHEER UP AND SMILE (1930)

Director: Sidney Lanfield

Produced by: Fox

Starring: Dixie Lee
Arthur Lake
with Duke Morrison in a bit part

THE BIG TRAIL (1930)

Director: Raoul Walsh

Produced by: Fox

Starring: John Wayne
Marguerite Churchill

GIRLS DEMAND EXCITEMENT (1931)

Director: Seymour Felix

Produced by: Fox

Starring: Virginia Cherrill
John Wayne
Marguerite Churchill

THREE GIRLS LOST (1931)

Director: Sidney Lanfield

Produced by: Fox

Starring: Loretta Young
John Wayne

MEN ARE LIKE THAT (1931)

Director: George B. Seitz

Produced by: Columbia Pictures

Starring: Laura LaPlante
John Wayne

THE DECEIVER (1931)

Director: Louis King

Produced by: Columbia Pictures

Starring: Lloyd Hughes
Dorothy Sebastian
with John Wayne playing a corpse

RANGE FEUD (1931)

Director: D. Ross Lederman
Produced by: Columbia Pictures
Starring: Buck Jones
           John Wayne

MAKER OF MEN (1931)

Director: Edward Sedgwick
Produced by: Columbia Pictures
Starring: Jack Holt
           with John Wayne as Dusty

SHADOW OF THE EAGLE (1932)

Director: Ford Beebe
Produced by: Mascot
Starring: John Wayne
           Dorothy Gulliver
           Edward Hearn

TEXAS CYCLONE (1932)

Director: D. Ross Lederman
Produced by: Columbia Pictures
Starring: Tim McCoy
           John Wayne

TWO FISTED LAW (1932)

Director: D. Ross Lederman
Produced by: Columbia Pictures
Starring: Tim McCoy
           Alice Day
           John Wayne

LADY AND GENT (1932)

Director: Stephen Roberts
Produced by: Paramount
Starring: George Bancroft
           Charles Starrett
           John Wayne

THE HURRICANE EXPRESS (1932)

Director: Armand Schaefer

Produced by: Mascot

Starring: John Wayne
               Shirley Grey
               Tully Marshall

RIDE HIM COWBOY (1932)

Director: Fred Allen

Produced by: Warner Bros.

Starring: John Wayne
               Ruth Hall

THE BIG STAMPEDE (1932)

Director: Tenny Wright

Produced by: Warner Bros.

Starring: John Wayne
               Noah Beery
               Mae Madison

HAUNTED GOLD (1932)

Director: Mack V. Wright

Produced by: Warner Bros.

Starring: John Wayne
               Sheila Terry

THE TELEGRAPH TRAIL (1933)

Director: Tenny Wright

Produced by: Warner Bros.

Starring: John Wayne
               Marceline Day
               Frank McHugh

THE THREE MUSKETEERS (1933)

Director: Armand Schaefer

Produced by: Mascot

Starring: John Wayne
               Ruth Hall
               Jack Mulhall
               Raymond Hatton

SOMEWHERE IN SONORA (1933)

Director: Mack V. Wright
Produced by: Warner Bros.
Starring: John Wayne
               Shirley Palmer

HIS PRIVATE SECRETARY (1933)

Director: Philip H. Whitman
Produced by: Showmen's Pictures
Starring: John Wayne
               Evalyn Knapp

BABY FACE (1933)

Director: Alfred E. Green
Produced by: Warner Bros.
Starring: Barbara Stanwyck
               George Brent
               with John Wayne as Jimmy McCoy

THE MAN FROM MONTEREY (1933)

Director: Mack V. Wright
Produced by: Warner Bros.
Starring: John Wayne
               Ruth Hall

RIDERS OF DESTINY (1933)

Director: R.N. Bradbury
Produced by: Lone Star
Starring: John Wayne
               Cecelia Parker

COLLEGE COACH (1933)

Director: William A. Wellman
Produced by: Warner Bros.
Starring: Pat O'Brien
               Ann Dvorak
               with John Wayne in a minor role

SAGEBRUSH TRAIL (1933)

Director: Armand Schaefer

Produced by: Lone Star

Starring: John Wayne
Nancy Shubert

THE LUCKY TEXAN (1934)

Director: R.N. Bradbury

Produced by: Lone Star

Starring: John Wayne
Barbara Sheldon

WEST OF THE DIVIDE (1934)

Director: R.N. Bradbury

Produced by: Lone Star

Starring: John Wayne
Virginia Browne Faire

BLUE STEEL (1934)

Director: R.N. Bradbury

Produced by: Lone Star

Starring: John Wayne
Eleanor Hunt

THE MAN FROM UTAH (1934)

Director: R.N. Bradbury

Produced by: Lone Star

Starring: John Wayne
Polly Ann Young

RANDY RIDES ALONE (1934)

Director: Harry Fraser

Produced by: Lone Star

Starring: John Wayne
Alberta Vaughn

THE STAR PACKER (1934)

Director: R.N. Bradbury

Produced by: Lone Star

Starring: John Wayne
Verna Hillie

THE TRAIL BEYOND (1934)

Director: R.N. Bradbury

Produced by: Lone Star

Starring: John Wayne
Noah Beery
Noah Beery, Jr.

THE LAWLESS FRONTIER (1934)

Director: R.N. Bradbury

Produced by: Lone Star

Starring: John Wayne
Sheila Terry

'NEATH ARIZONA SKIES (1934)

Director: Harry Fraser

Produced by: Lone Star

Starring: John Wayne
Sheila Terry

TEXAS TERROR (1935)

Director: R.N. Bradbury

Produced by: Lone Star

Starring: John Wayne
Lucille Brown

RAINBOW VALLEY (1935)

Director: R.N. Bradbury

Produced by: Lone Star

Starring: John Wayne
Lucille Brown

THE DESERT TRAIL (1935)

Director: Cullen Lewis
Produced by: Lone Star
Starring: John Wayne
           Mary Kornman

THE DAWN RIDER (1935)

Director: R.N. Bradbury
Produced by: Monogram
Starring: John Wayne
           Marion Burns

PARADISE CANYON (1935)

Director: Carl Pierson
Produced by: Monogram
Starring: John Wayne
           Marion Burns

WESTWARD HO (1935)

Director: R.N. Bradbury
Produced by: Republic
Starring: John Wayne
           Sheila Manners

THE NEW FRONTIER (1935)

Director: Carl Pierson
Produced by: Republic
Starring: John Wayne
           Muriel Evans

THE LAWLESS RANGE (1935)

Director: R.N. Bradbury
Produced by: Republic
Starring: John Wayne
           Sheila Manners

THE OREGON TRAIL (1936)

Director: Scott Pembroke
Produced by: Republic
Starring: John Wayne
               Ann Rutherford

THE LAWLESS NINETIES (1936)

Director: Joseph Kane
Produced by: Republic
Starring: John Wayne
               Ann Rutherford

KING OF THE PECOS (1936)

Director: Joseph Kane
Produced by: Republic
Starring: John Wayne
               Muriel Evans

THE LONELY TRAIL (1936)

Director: Joseph Kane
Produced by: Republic
Starring: John Wayne
               Ann Rutherford

WINDS OF THE WASTELAND (1936)

Director: Mack V. Wright
Produced by: Republic
Starring: John Wayne
               Phyllis Fraser

THE SEA SPOILERS (1936)

Director: Frank Strayer
Produced by: Universal
Starring: John Wayne
               Nan Grey

CONFLICT (1936)

Director: David Howard

Produced by: Universal

Starring: John Wayne
Jean Rogers

CALIFORNIA STRAIGHT AHEAD (1937)

Director: Arthur Lubin

Produced by: Universal

Starring: John Wayne
Louise Latimer

I COVER THE WAR (1937)

Director: Arthur Lubin

Produced by: Universal

Starring: John Wayne
Gwen Gaze

IDOL OF THE CROWDS (1937)

Director: Arthur Lubin

Produced by: Universal

Starring: John Wayne
Sheila Bromley

ADVENTURE'S END (1937)

Director: Arthur Lubin

Produced by: Universal

Starring: John Wayne
Diana Gibson
Montagu Love

BORN TO THE WEST (1937)

Director: Charles Barton

Produced by: Paramount

Starring: John Wayne
Marsha Hunt
with Alan Ladd in a bit part

PALS OF THE SADDLE (1938)

Director: George Sherman
Produced by: Republic
Starring: John Wayne
Ray Corrigan
Max Terhune

OVERLAND STAGE RAIDERS (1938)

Director: George Sherman
Produced by: Republic
Starring: John Wayne
Ray Corrigan
Max Terhune

SANTA FE STAMPEDE (1938)

Director: George Sherman
Produced by: Republic
Starring: John Wayne
Ray Corrigan
Max Terhune

RED RIVER RANGE (1938)

Director: George Sherman
Produced by: Republic
Starring: John Wayne
Ray Corrigan
Max Terhune

STAGECOACH (1939)

Director: John Ford
Produced by: Walter Wanger Productions
Starring: Claire Trevor
John Wayne
John Carradine
Thomas Mitchell
Andy Devine
Donald Meek

THE NIGHT RIDERS (1939)

Director: George Sherman

Produced by: Republic

Starring: John Wayne
Ray Corrigan
Max Terhune

THREE TEXAS STEERS (1939)

Director: George Sherman

Produced by: Republic

Starring: John Wayne
Ray Corrigan
Max Terhune
and introducing Carole Landis

WYOMING OUTLAW (1939)

Director: George Sherman

Produced by: Republic

Starring: John Wayne
Ray Corrigan
Raymond Hatton

NEW FRONTIER (1939)

Director: George Sherman

Produced by: Republic

Starring: John Wayne
Ray Corrigan
Raymond Hatton
with Phyllis Isley who later became
Jennifer Jones

ALLEGHENY UPRISING (1939)

Director: William A. Seiter

Produced by: RKO Radio

Starring: Claire Trevor
John Wayne
George Sanders
Brian Donlevy

THE DARK COMMAND (1940)

Director: Raoul Walsh

Second Unit: Yakima Canutt

Produced by: Republic

Starring: Claire Trevor
John Wayne
Walter Pidgeon
Roy Rogers

THREE FACES WEST (1940)

Director: Bernard Vorhaus

Produced by: Republic

Starring: John Wayne
Charles Coburn
Sigrid Gurie

THE LONG VOYAGE HOME (1940)

Director: John Ford

Produced by: Walter Wanger Productions

Starring: John Wayne
Thomas Mitchell
Barry Fitzgerald
Mildred Natwick

SEVEN SINNERS (1940)

Director: Tay Garnett

Produced by: Universal

Starring: Marlene Dietrich
John Wayne
Albert Dekker

A MAN BETRAYED (1941)

Director: John A. Auer

Produced by: Republic

Starring: John Wayne
Frances Dee

LADY FROM LOUISIANA (1941)

Director: Bernard Vorhaus

Produced by: Republic

Starring: John Wayne
                Ona Munson

THE SHEPHERD OF THE HILLS (1941)

Director: Henry Hathaway

Produced by: Paramount

Starring: John Wayne
                Betty Field
                Harry Carey

LADY FOR A NIGHT (1942)

Director: Leigh Jason

Produced by: Republic

Starring: Joan Blondell
                John Wayne

REAP THE WILD WIND (1942)

Director: Cecil B. DeMille

Produced by: Cecil B. DeMille for Paramount

Starring: Ray Milland
                John Wayne
                Paulette Goddard
                Raymond Massey
                Robert Preston
                Susan Hayward

THE SPOILERS (1942)

Director: Ray Enright

Produced by: Universal

Starring: Marlene Dietrich
                Randolph Scott
                John Wayne

IN OLD CALIFORNIA (1942)

Director: William McGann

Produced by: Republic

Starring: John Wayne
Binnie Barnes
Albert Dekker
Helen Parrish

FLYING TIGERS (1942)

Director: David Miller

Produced by: Republic

Starring: John Wayne
John Carroll
Anna Lee
Paul Kelly

REUNION IN FRANCE (1942)

Director: Jules Dassin

Produced by: MGM

Starring: Joan Crawford
John Wayne
with Philip Dorn and Reginald Owen

PITTSBURGH (1942)

Director: Lewis Seiler

Produced by: Universal

Starring: Marlene Dietrich
Randolph Scott
John Wayne

A LADY TAKES A CHANCE (1943)

Director: William A. Seiter

Produced by: RKO Radio

Starring: Jean Arthur
John Wayne

IN OLD OKLAHOMA (1943)

Director: Albert S. Rogell

Produced by: Republic

Starring: John Wayne
                Martha Scott
                Albert Dekker

THE FIGHTING SEABEES (1944)

Director: Edward Ludwig

Produced by: Republic

Starring: John Wayne
                Dennis O'Keefe
                Susan Hayward

TALL IN THE SADDLE (1944)

Director: Edwin L. Marin

Produced by: Robert Fellows for RKO Radio

Starring: John Wayne
                Ella Raines
                with Ward Bond

FLAME OF THE BARBARY COAST (1945)

Director: Joseph Kane

Produced by: Republic

Starring: John Wayne
                Ann Dvorak
                with Joseph Schildkraut and William Frawley

BACK TO BATAAN (1945)

Director: Edward Dmytryk

Produced by: Robert Fellows for RKO Radio

Starring: John Wayne
                Anthony Quinn
                with Beulah Bondi

THEY WERE EXPENDABLE (1945)

Director: John Ford

Produced by: John Ford for MGM

Starring: Robert Montgomery
John Wayne
Donna Reed
with Jack Holt and Ward Bond

DAKOTA (1945)

Director: Joseph Kane

Produced by: Republic

Starring: John Wayne
Vera Hruba Ralston
Walter Brennan
with Ward Bond, Mike Mazurki and Ona Munson

WITHOUT RESERVATIONS (1946)

Director: Mervyn LeRoy

Produced by: RKO Radio

Starring: Claudette Colbert
John Wayne
Don DeFore
with Anne Triola

ANGEL AND THE BADMAN (1947)

Director: James Edward Grant

Produced by: John Wayne for Republic

Starring: John Wayne
Gail Russell

TYCOON (1947)

Director: Richard Wallace

Produced by: RKO Radio

Starring: John Wayne
Laraine Day
Sir Cedric Hardwicke
Judith Anderson
with James Gleason and Anthony Quinn

FORT APACHE (1948)

Director: John Ford

Produced by: John Ford and Merian C. Cooper for RKO Radio

Starring: John Wayne
Henry Fonda
Shirley Temple
Pedro Armendariz
John Agar
with Ward Bond and Victor McLaglen

RED RIVER (1948)

Director: Howard Hawks

Produced by: Howard Hawks for United Artists

Starring: John Wayne
Montgomery Clift
Joanne Dru
Walter Brennan
with John Ireland and Mickey Kuhn

THREE GODFATHERS (1949)

Director: John Ford

Produced by: John Ford and Merian C. Cooper for MGM

Starring: John Wayne
Pedro Armendariz
Harry Carey, Jr.
with Ward Bond and Mildred Natwick

WAKE OF THE RED WITCH (1949)

Director: Edward Ludwig

Produced by: Republic

Starring: John Wayne
Gail Russell
Gig Young
with Adele Mara and Luther Adler

THE FIGHTING KENTUCKIAN (1949)

Director: George Waggner

Produced by: John Wayne for Republic

Starring: John Wayne
Vera Hruba Ralston
with Philip Dorn, John Howard and Hugo Haas

SHE WORE A YELLOW RIBBON (1949)

Director: John Ford

Produced by: John Ford and Merian C. Cooper for RKO Radio

Starring: John Wayne
Joanne Dru
John Agar
Ben Johnson
Harry Carey, Jr.
with Victor McLaglen and Mildred Natwick

SANDS OF IWO JIMA (1949)

Director: Allan Dwan

Produced by: Republic

Starring: John Wayne
John Agar
Adele Mara
Forrest Tucker
with Martin Milner

RIO GRANDE (1950)

Director: John Ford

Produced by: John Ford and Merian C. Cooper for Republic

Starring: John Wayne
Maureen O'Hara
Ben Johnson
with J. Carrol Naish and Victor McLaglen

OPERATION PACIFIC (1951)

Director: George Waggner

Produced by: Warner Bros.

Starring: John Wayne
Patricia Neal
with Ward Bond

FLYING LEATHERNECKS (1951)

Director: Nicholas Ray

Produced by: RKO Radio

Starring: John Wayne
Robert Ryan
with Adam Williams

THE QUIET MAN (1952)

Director: John Ford

Produced by: John Ford and Merian C. Cooper for Republic

Starring: John Wayne
Maureen O'Hara
Barry Fitzgerald
Ward Bond
Victor McLaglen

BIG JIM McLAIN (1952)

Director: Edward Ludwig

Produced by: Wayne-Fellows for Warner Bros.

Starring: John Wayne
Nancy Olson
with James Arness

TROUBLE ALONG THE WAY (1953)

Director: Michael Curtiz

Produced by: Warner Bros.

Starring: John Wayne
Donna Reed

ISLAND IN THE SKY (1953)

Director: William A. Wellman

Produced by: Wayne-Fellows for Warner Bros.

Starring: John Wayne
Lloyd Nolan
Walter Abel
with Sean McClory

HONDO (1953)

Director: John Farrow

Produced by: Wayne-Fellows for Warner Bros.

Starring: John Wayne
Geraldine Page

THE HIGH AND THE MIGHTY (1954)

Director: William A. Wellman

Produced by: Wayne-Fellows for Warner Bros.

Starring: John Wayne
Claire Trevor
Laraine Day
Robert Stack

THE SEA CHASE (1955)

Director: John Farrow

Produced by: Warner Bros.

Starring: John Wayne
Lana Turner
with Lyle Bettger

BLOOD ALLEY (1955)

Director: William A. Wellman

Produced by: Batjac for Warner Bros.

Starring: John Wayne
Lauren Bacall
with Anita Ekberg

THE CONQUEROR (1956)

Director: Dick Powell

Produced by: RKO Radio

Starring: John Wayne
Susan Hayward

THE SEARCHERS (1956)

Director: John Ford

Produced by: Merian C. Cooper and C. V. Whitney
for Warner Bros.

Starring: John Wayne
Jeffrey Hunter
Vera Miles

THE WINGS OF EAGLES (1957)

Director: John Ford

Produced by: MGM

Starring: John Wayne
Maureen O'Hara
Dan Dailey
with Ken Curtis and Kenneth Tobey

JET PILOT (1957)

Director: Josef von Sternberg

Produced by: Howard Hughes/RKO Radio

Starring: John Wayne
Janet Leigh

LEGEND OF THE LOST (1957)

Director: Henry Hathaway

Produced by: Batjac for United Artists

Starring: John Wayne
Sophia Loren
Rossano Brazzi

THE BARBARIAN AND THE GEISHA (1958)

Director: John Huston

Produced by: 20th Century-Fox

Starring: John Wayne
Eiko Ando
Sam Jaffe

RIO BRAVO (1959)

Director: Howard Hawks

Produced by: Howard Hawks for Warner Bros.

Starring: John Wayne
Dean Martin
Ricky Nelson
Angie Dickinson
with Walter Brennan and Ward Bond

THE HORSE SOLDIERS (1959)

Director: John Ford

Produced by: John Lee Mahin and Martin Rackin for United Artists

Starring: John Wayne
William Holden

THE ALAMO (1960)

Director: John Wayne

Produced by: Batjac for United Artists

Starring: John Wayne
Richard Widmark
Laurence Harvey
Richard Boone

NORTH TO ALASKA (1960)

Director: Henry Hathaway

Produced by: Henry Hathaway for 20th Century-Fox

Starring: John Wayne
Stewart Granger

THE COMANCHEROS (1961)

Director: Michael Curtiz

Produced by: 20th Century-Fox

Starring: John Wayne
Stuart Whitman

THE MAN WHO SHOT LIBERTY VALANCE (1962)

Director: John Ford

Produced by: John Ford Prods. for Paramount

Starring: James Stewart
John Wayne
Vera Miles
Lee Marvin
with Edmond O'Brien and Strother Martin

HATARI (1962)

Director:	Howard Hawks
Produced by:	Howard Hawks for Paramount
Starring:	John Wayne
	Elsa Martinelli

HOW THE WEST WAS WON (1962)

Director:	John Ford
Produced by:	MGM
Starring:	John Wayne as General William T. Sherman

THE LONGEST DAY (1963)

Director:	Darryl F. Zanuck
Produced by:	Darryl F. Zanuck for 20th Century-Fox
Starring:	John Wayne in a cameo role

DONOVAN'S REEF (1963)

Director:	John Ford
Produced by:	John Ford for Paramount
Starring:	John Wayne
	Lee Marvin

McLINTOCK! (1963)

Director:	Andrew V. McLaglen
Produced by:	Batjac for United Artists
Starring:	John Wayne
	Maureen O'Hara
	Yvonne De Carlo
	with Patrick Wayne

CIRCUS WORLD (1964)

Director:	Henry Hathaway
Produced by:	Paramount
Starring:	John Wayne
	Claudia Cardinale
	Rita Hayworth

THE GREATEST STORY EVER TOLD (1965)

Director: George Stevens
Produced by: George Stevens for United Artists
Starring: John Wayne in a cameo role

IN HARM'S WAY (1965)

Director: Otto Preminger
Produced by: Otto Preminger for Paramount
Starring: John Wayne
Kirk Douglas
Patricia Neal

THE SONS OF KATIE ELDER (1965)

Director: Henry Hathaway
Produced by: Hal Wallis for Paramount
Starring: John Wayne
Dean Martin
Martha Hyer
Michael Anderson, Jr.
Earl Holliman

CAST A GIANT SHADOW (1966)

Director: Melville Shavelson
Produced by: Melville Shavelson and Michael Wayne
for United Artists
Starring: John Wayne
Kirk Douglas
Angie Dickinson
with Frank Sinatra

THE WAR WAGON (1967)

Director: Burt Kennedy
Produced by: Batjac for Universal
Starring: John Wayne
Kirk Douglas
with Howard Keel and Robert Walker

EL DORADO (1967)

Director: Howard Hawks

Produced by: Howard Hawks for Paramount

Starring: John Wayne
                Robert Mitchum
                James Caan

THE GREEN BERETS (1968)

Director: John Wayne

Produced by: Batjac for Warner Bros.—Seven Arts

Starring: John Wayne
                David Janssen
                with Jack Soo, Bruce Cabot and Irene Tsu

HELLFIGHTERS (1969)

Director: Andrew V. McLaglen

Produced by: Universal

Starring: John Wayne
                Katharine Ross

TRUE GRIT (1969)

Director: Henry Hathaway

Produced by: Hal Wallis for Paramount

Starring: John Wayne
                Glen Campbell
                Kim Darby

THE UNDEFEATED (1969)

Director: Andrew V. McLaglen

Produced by: 20th Century-Fox

Starring: John Wayne
                Rock Hudson

CHISUM (1970)

Director: Andrew V. McLaglen

Produced by: Batjac for Warner Bros.

Starring: John Wayne
Forrest Tucker
Christopher George

RIO LOBO (1970)

Director: Howard Hawks

Produced by: Howard Hawks

Starring: John Wayne
Jorge Rivero
Jennifer O'Neill
with Victor French

BIG JAKE (1971)

Director: George Sherman

Produced by: Batjac

Starring: John Wayne
Richard Boone
Maureen O'Hara
with Patrick Wayne and John Ethan Wayne

THE COWBOYS (1972)

Director: Mark Rydell

Produced by: Mark Rydell for Warner Bros.

Starring: John Wayne
Roscoe Lee Browne
Bruce Dern

THE TRAIN ROBBERS (1973)

Director: Burt Kennedy

Produced by: Batjac for Warner Bros.

Starring: John Wayne
Ann-Margret
with Rod Taylor and Ben Johnson

CAHILL, UNITED STATES MARSHAL (1973)

Director: Andrew V. McLaglen
Produced by: Batjac for Warner Bros.
Starring: John Wayne
             George Kennedy

McQ (1974)

Director: John Sturges
Produced by: Batjac/Levy-Gardner for Warner Bros.
Starring: John Wayne
             Eddie Albert

BRANNIGAN (1975)

Director: Douglas Hickox
Produced by: Wellborn for United Artists
Starring: John Wayne
             Richard Attenborough
             Mel Ferrer

ROOSTER COGBURN (1975)

Director: Stuart Millar
Produced by: Hal Wallis for Universal
Starring: John Wayne
             Katharine Hepburn

THE SHOOTIST (1976)

Director: Don Siegel
Produced by: Dino De Laurentis for Paramount
Starring: John Wayne
             Lauren Bacall
             Ron Howard
             James Stewart

Index

A

B

C

E

F

I

N

O